The Library Reference Series

BASIC REFERENCE SOURCES

The Library Reference Series
Lee Ash
General Editor

AN INDEX TO INDEXES

*A Subject Bibliography
of Published Indexes*

By
NORMA OLIN IRELAND

GREGG PRESS
Boston 1972

This is a complete photographic reprint of a work
first published in Boston by The F. W. Faxon Company in 1942.
Reproduced from an original copy in the Teachers College Library.

First Gregg Press edition published 1972.

Printed on permanent/durable acid-free paper in
The United States of America.

Library of Congress Cataloging in Publication Data

Ireland, Norma (Olin), 1907-
   An index to indexes.

   (Library reference series)
   Reprint of the 1942 ed.
   1. Indexes--Bibliography. I. Title.
Z6293.I7 1972   016.016   72-8745
ISBN 0-8398-0855-0

USEFUL REFERENCE SERIES, No. 67

AN INDEX TO INDEXES

A SUBJECT BIBLIOGRAPHY OF PUBLISHED INDEXES

BY

NORMA OLIN IRELAND

Director, Ireland Indexing Service
El Monte, California

BOSTON
THE F. W. FAXON COMPANY
1942

Copyright by
The F. W. Faxon Company
1942

PRINTED IN THE UNITED STATES OF AMERICA

THE MURRAY PRINTING COMPANY
CAMBRIDGE, MASSACHUSETTS

TO
MY TWO SISTERS:

LUCRETIA OLIN ROWE
A missionary in the Belgian Congo, Africa

HALCYON OLIN HARPER
A teacher in Akron, Ohio

TABLE OF CONTENTS

	Page
PREFACE	xi
AN INDEX TO INDEXES	1
APPENDIX: FREQUENCY TABLE	75
AUTHOR-TITLE INDEX	78

PREFACE

Altho indexes, as separate publications, date their development only back to the nineteenth century, nevertheless they are, at the present time, essential tools of the library profession. How we once did without them we do not know; we do know, however, that we now use these timesavers daily in our work and that they are essential to its efficient accomplishment.

New indexes are appearing every year, especially in the field of books. Periodical indexes have had an earlier start and are now well-established, but the indexing of material found in books is really just beginning. Publishers and librarians are coöperating to accomplish such publications, and the strides made in this direction have been rapid.

PURPOSE AND SCOPE

Our purpose in this work is to assemble into one volume a selection of *published* indexes which will aid librarians and students who wish to quickly locate the index-sources of the various subject fields. It may also be used as a companion volume to the forthcoming "Local indexes in American libraries," compiled by the Junior Members Round Table of the American Library Association and now being edited by the writer. This latter work will list *unpublished* indexes located in American libraries.

It has been difficult to draw a clear line of demarcation between indexes and bibliographies. All indexes are of course bibliographies, but not all bibliographies are indexes. While in most cases we have attempted to interpret the word index in its strictest meaning, ("A table, list or file, usually arranged alphabetically, for facilitating reference to topics, names, objects, etc. especially in a book or a collection" — Webster) yet we have made some exceptions. We have included some few titles which are only bibliographies, for one of two reasons; (1) to complete the coverage of a certain subject for a period of years (i.e. **Tests, Mental**); (2) to bring out certain titles whose analytical indexes were especially valuable, thus making the work fall into this category (i.e. **Quotations**), indexes to certain catalogs (i.e. Standard catalog), and indexes to sets of books (i.e. **Encyclopedias**).

Five different types of indexes are incorporated: (1) Special indexes, (2) Indexes to sets of books, (3) Periodical indexes, (4) Cumulative indexes to individual periodicals, and (5) Government document indexes. They are not segregated under these headings, however, but are interfiled according to our plan of subject arrangement (see below).

With the exception of type number 1, special indexes, only American indexes are included, since the inclusion of English and foreign indexes of the other four types would lengthen this work beyond its purpose. In the case of special indexes, some English works were chosen because of their frequent and immediate use in most libraries. Thus we have attempted to select those indexes which would be found in the majority of libraries (see also Frequency table, and Periodicals) and those which have either current usage or historic value.

Frequency Table

At the suggestion of Dr. Louis Shores, Director of Peabody Library School of Nashville, Tennessee, we are including a "Frequency Table" in the appendix. This was compiled through the coöperation of reference librarians in representative public, university and college, teacher training and state libraries, chosen from representative sections of the United States. Indexes in the Frequency Table are starred throughout the work.

Arrangement and Scope

Over 1,000 separate indexes are listed in our work, under 280 different subjects. While the list is selective, it may also be called somewhat comprehensive, notwithstanding the fact that we have omitted several hundred titles which were in the original card file.

The arrangement is by subject, with an author-title index. The subject headings were chosen from no particular source, but were adapted from various sources for the special needs of this bibliography. While such headings as Books, Business and commerce, Periodicals, General, etc. might not be approved in general catalogs, nevertheless they are entirely adequate for our purpose. We have included cross-references when necessary.

Bibliographic Information

Author, title, publisher and place of publication, date, and pages are given for each book. Price is not indicated because this work is not intended primarily as a buying list (altho of course it can be used to check library holdings and build up a collection),

AN INDEX TO INDEXES

and many out-of-print titles are included. Annotations are likewise excluded because, for most of the indexes such as periodicals, they would be neither necessary nor desirable. Uniformity seemed preferable.

Information for cumulative indexes of periodicals includes name of periodical, place of publication, volumes and dates. Altho some of these are published separately, the majority are issued as part of the magazines which they index, and thus further bibliographic information is nonessential. In the case of indexes to proceedings of societies, etc., the same procedure is followed; a few titles do not give place of publication however, as publication is often "let out" to highest bidder and thus names of press and locality do not appear.

To our knowledge there are only five published lists of cumulative indexes to periodicals (one of which is still in press), all of which are arranged by title rather than subject. We thot, therefore, a subject list would also be useful since the value of such lists was evident. In regard to their usefulness, Miss Isadore Mudge says:[1] "... while most of the periodicals are indexed in periodical indexes, nevertheless approach is not always the same as for detailed subject interest. Years covered are not always complete in periodical indexes, and information is not always complete (e.g. I.A.I.: does not give author entries of articles)."

The primary bases for selection of these individual periodicals were the aforementioned lists, as follows:

(1–3) Roys, Margaret, comp. Separate indexes to individual periodicals
 In International index, 1924–1927, p.v–x.
 International index, 1928–1931, p.v–xi.
 International index, 1931–1934, p.v–xiv.
(4) Cumulative indexes to individual periodicals (by Margaret Roys)
 In Bibliographic index, v.1, p333ff. 1939.
(5) Haskell, Daniel C. A checklist of cumulative indexes to individual periodicals in the New York public library. N. Y., N. Y. public library. (In press.)

Union lists were likewise a source of information, as they showed the frequency of certain periodicals in representative areas. The following were especially used:

Gregory, Winifred. Union list of serials (and supplements). N. Y., Wilson.
N. Y. Special libraries. Union list of special libraries of N. Y. metropolitan district. 1931.
Special libraries assoc. of Southern California chapter. Union list of periodicals in libraries of Southern California. 3d ed. rev. and enl. 1941.
Special libraries asso. of San Francisco Bay Region chapter. Union list of serials in San Francisco Bay Region, . 1939.

[1] International index, 1924–1926, p. v.

Cumulative indexes to individual English and foreign periodicals were excluded, not only because of the prohibitive increase in this work which their inclusion would entail, but also because of their infrequent use in the average library. The general indexes to periodicals, especially *International index*, were thot sufficient to cover the use of such periodicals. On the other hand, indexes to older American indexes, now discontinued, and early indexes to current periodicals are both included, not only for their historic value but also because *Poole* and other indexes did not include, or if they did, the information given was too brief.

A few annual indexes are included such as *Life*, where no cumulative index has yet been published, and the annual index is indispensable. This is also the case with some government documents. It must be remembered, tho, that while annual indexes are not usually included in this list, yet they should be used in connection with the cumulative indexes in order to bring the latter up-to-date.

Use of Indexes

An important consideration in the use of indexes is the necessity of making them readily accessible to students and other patrons of the library, as well as convenient to the librarian. The most efficient method of displaying and shelving indexes is by means of the *Index Table*. While a table intended primarily for periodical indexes is usually considered sufficient, we should like to suggest that such a table be made to include special book indexes as well. Many librarians segregate a few such indexes for ready reference at their desk, but why not place them where patrons can also benefit? Perhaps a few extra shelves need be added, but the expense would be negligible. Some librarians may say that patrons cannot always use such indexes to the best advantage, but we have proven, in three different libraries, that with a little guidance patrons (including students) soon learn to use these indexes at the index table *easily* and *well*. The reference librarian will soon find that her work will be lightened in many instances by this arrangement, and more intelligent users of the library will be the result of her efforts.

For those unfamiliar with the construction of the index table, perhaps a word of explanation might be useful. The table consists of 2 rows of double-faced shelves, built up from the center of a regular library table. The indexes may be distributed on both sides, according to their use. When special book indexes are to be included, it is suggested that the upper section be reserved for them, and the periodical indexes placed on the lower section because of their size. Obviously, all indexes cannot be thus segregated (for instance, indexes to sets of books), but at least the most useful and popular can be included. "Sketches of two tables designed for library use — one for magazine indexes and the other for such tools as the *United States Catalog* have been sent to A.L.A. headquarters by members of the committee on library equipment and appliances. They may be borrowed, upon request, from the library at A.L.A. headquarters," according to a notice in the *A.L.A. Bulletin* a few years ago.[2] We presume this information is still available. Pictures and descriptions of similar tables appear in various *Wilson Library Bulletin* articles.[3][4]

AUTHORITIES; ACKNOWLEDGMENTS

No exact list of authorities is possible because the sources for this work are multitudinous! While of course the most important ones are the recognized lists of reference books *Mudge*, (*Shores, Winchell*), government documents (*Boyd, Schmeckebier, Wilcox*), periodicals (*Haskell, Roys*), yet every library catalog, every publisher's trade catalog was a possible source for indexes. For over *seven* years we *collected* indexes; it was a hobby for spare hours and evenings! But, as Mr. Faxon wrote us in 1935: "such a subject can never be complete no matter how long you wait or how diligently you search." When, therefore, a comprehensive list proved infeasible, the job of *selection* became necessary.

Selection in special subject fields would likewise have been an impossible task without the aid of fellow librarians, librarians who are specialists in their own subject fields, and whose help we greatly appreciate. As a former reference librarian, we also appreciate the cooperation of librarians in Southern California who made their reference services easily available to us, and in some instances even *loaned* us *reference books* for home use! Therefore we wish to take this opportunity to thank those librarians and others for their willing assistance. We wish to say, however, that we assume *full*

[2] Drawings of library furniture. A.L.A. Bulletin 12:849 Dec. 1935.
[3] An attractive index table. Wilson Bulletin 6:283 Dec. 1931.
[4] Advertising our time-savers. Wilson Bulletin 9:371. Mr. 1935.

AN INDEX TO INDEXES

responsibility for errors in *all* subject fields, since our advisers did not see the finished work, which necessarily contained some changes from their original suggestions.

DR. LOUIS SHORES, Director of Peabody Library School, Nashville, Tenn., for the great amount of time spent in examining our cards, and for his splendid suggestions especially in the field of Education.

MISS MARGARET ROYS, Assistant supervisor, Catalog dept., in charge of serials, Columbia university libraries, N. Y. city, for her generous loan of current periodical index cards, supplementing her published lists, and also for her revision of many of our own cards. MR. JOHN CONNOR, of the Columbia university medical library, for his suggestions on Medicine.

MR. DANIEL HASKELL, Bibliographer of the New York public library, for solving many problems regarding periodical indexes, and for his willingness to pass on information contained in his bibliography before its publication.

MR. THOMAS DABAGH, Law librarian of the Los Angeles Co. law library, for his detailed advice and suggested arrangement of Law indexes.

MISS MARION EWING, Assistant librarian of the Pomona College library, Claremont, California, for making easily available government document and other indexes contained in the splendid collection of that library. We also appreciate her loan of several reference books.

MISS HELEN COWLES, Reference librarian of the Claremont Colleges library, for extending the use of all reference services in that library.

MISS ALTHEA WARREN, Librarian of the Los Angeles public library, for granting permission for the use of special services and collections. We also thank the staff of the Teachers dept. of L.A.P.L. for their always-willing service, especially MISS ROSEMARY LIVSEY, head of department, and MR. ARMINE MCKENZIE, assistant in the department. MRS. PAOTA WHITE PATRICK, of the Genealogical department of the Los Angeles public library, for her suggestions on Genealogy.

MRS. FRANCES DAVIS, Librarian of the Bureau of Power and Light Library, Los Angeles, for the loan of a reference book; MISS EVELYN HUSTON, Librarian of the Bureau of Governmental Research, University of California at Los Angeles, for a similar loan.

The University of Southern California School of Library Service class of 1938, for their "hunting out" additional indexes in connection with the Reference course during the 2d semester of that year. GUIDO FERRARI, chairman of the Index committee, for his good work.

DAVID E. IRELAND, my husband, who as a statistician and graduate student gave me his criticism on the use of such a list, and assisted in the compilation of the Frequency Table reports.

The Reference librarians who so willingly coöperated in the Frequency Table.

AN INDEX TO INDEXES
On Frequency Table (See Appendix)

Accidents, Industrial

International association of industrial accident boards and commissions. Proceedings. Index... 1914–1924, by Glenn L. Tibbott. Wash., D. C., 1925. 57p. (Also in U. S. Bureau of labor statistics bulletin 295:1–57, 1925).

U. S. Dept. of labor. Cumulative loose-leaf index to the Proceedings of the International association of industrial accident boards and commissions, prepared by J. William O'Connell. (Bulletin no. 29.) Wash., D. C., Govt. print. off., 1939.

Accounting

American institute of accountants. Accountants' index. N. Y., The Institute, 1921–date. Basic volume — 1912–1920.

Supplements: 1. 1921–1923
2. 1923–1927
3. 1928–1934
4. 1932–1935
5. 1936–1939

The Journal of accountancy. N. Y., American institute of accountancy. Index, v. 1–16, 1905–1914; v. 17–34, 1914–1922.

National association of cost accountants. Bulletin. N. Y., The Association. Complete topical index, N.A.C.A. publications, April 1920–Feb. 1, 1939, Section III. (In v. 20, no. 11, p. 699–766.)

Selby, Paul Owen, comp. Index to the teaching of bookkeeping and accounting; a 10-year bibliography, 1929–1938. Kirksville, Mo., Research press, 1939. 44p.

U. S. General accounting office. Index-digest of the Comptroller general of the U. S. with statutes, decisions, and opinions, 1929–1940. Wash., Govt. print. off., 1941. 1078p.

U. S. General accounting office. Index to the published decisions... with statutes, decisions, and opinions cited therein... 1894–1929. Wash., D. C., Govt. print. off., 1931. 875p. (A compilation of the indexes appearing in the 27 volumes of the Decisions of the Comptroller of the treasury, and v. 1–8 of Decisions of the Comptroller general of U. S.)

Acoustics

Acoustical society of America. The journal. Lancaster, Pa., Published for the Acoustical society of America by the American institute of physics. Cumulative index, v. 1–10. 1929–1939.

Aeronautics

Aeronautical reader's guide. N. Y. Published quarterly for the Aeronautical archives by the Institute of the aeronautical sciences. v. 1–date, Sept. 1940–date.

U. S. Library of congress. Division of aeronautics. Subject index to aeronautical periodical literature and reports . . . 1938–date. Compiled by the Division of aeronautics, Library of congress, issued in coöperation with the Institute of the aeronautical science. N. Y., 1939–date.

U. S. Works progress administration. Bibliography of aeronautics . . . compiled from the Index of aeronautics of the Institute of aeronautical sciences. N. Y. 1936–1940 (pt. 1, 1938), pts. 1–2, 4–44, 46–50 and supplement to pts. 1–3, 11.

Africa, South

South African library association. Index to South African periodicals, *see* Periodicals.

Agricultural Chemistry

See also Soils.

Association of official agricultural chemists. Journal. Wash., D. C., The Association. Index, 1884–1929. (Caption title reads: Index of the Proceedings.)

Agricultural Education

U. S. Office of education. An annotated bibliography of 373 studies in agricultural education with a classified subject index and a general evaluation. (Vocational education bulletin 180; Agricultural series 18.) Wash., D. C., Govt. print. off., 1935. 196p.

Agriculture

See also Agricultural Chemistry; Agricultural Education; Botany; Entomology; Forests and Forestry; Lands; Soils.

*Agricultural index, subject index to a selected list of agricultural periodicals and bulletins, 1916–date. N. Y., Wilson co., 1919–date.

American society of agronomy. Journal. Geneva, N. Y. General index, v. 1–20, 1907–1928; author and subject index, v. 21–30 inclusive, 1929–1938.

Bailey, Liberty Hyde. Standard cyclopedia of horticulture. N. Y. Macmillan, 1914–1917. (Last volume is index. Includes full indexing and illustrations.)

Cornell countryman. Ithaca, N. Y., Cornell university. College of agriculture. Index, v. 1–3, 1903–1906.

Farm economics. Ithaca, N. Y., Cornell university. Index, no. 77–96. (*In* no. 96, p. 2356–2364. 1936.)

Iowa state agricultural society. Report. Index, v. 1–24, 1854–1877.

Irrigation age. Chicago. Index, v. 1–4, 1891–1893.

Journal of farm economics. Menasha, Wisconsin. Index, v. 1–10, 1919–1928; v. 11–20, 1929–1938.

Massachusetts. Agricultural experiment station. Amherst, Mass. Index, bulletins and reports, 1888–1907.

Society for the promotion of agricultural science. Proceedings. Syracuse, N. Y. Index, v. 1–16, 1880–1899.

U. S. Animal industry bureau. Index to literature relating to animal husbandry in the publications of the U. S. Department of agriculture, 1837–1898, by George Fayette Thompson. (Publications division bulletin 5.) Wash., D. C., Govt. print. off., 1900. 676p.

U. S. Bureau of agricultural economics. Library. Indexes to state official sources of agricultural statistics. (Agricultural economic bibliography no. 15, 21, 31.) Wash., D. C., Govt. print. off., 1931. 5v.

U. S. Crop estimates bureau. Statistical data compiled and published by the Bureau, 1863–1920. (Dept. of agriculture circular, 150.) Wash., D. C., Govt. print. off., 1921. 64p. (Part 2 — Subjects included in the reports and records of the Bureau.)

U. S. Dept. of agriculture. Index to authors with titles of their publications, appearing in the documents of the U. S. Dept. of agriculture, 1841–1897, by George F. Thompson. (Publications division bulletin 4.) Wash., D. C., Govt. print. off., 1898. 303p.

U. S. Dept. of agriculture. Index to Department bulletins, no. 1–1500, by Mabel G. Hunt . . . Wash., D. C., Govt. print. off., 1936. 384p.

*U. S. Dept. of agriculture. Index to Farmer's bulletins, 1–1000, compiled by C. H. Greathouse. Wash., D. C., Govt. print. off., 1920. 811p.

*U. S. Dept. of agriculture. Index to Farmer's bulletins, 1001–1500, compiled by Mabel G. Hunt. Wash., D. C., Govt. print. off., 1929. 371p.

*U. S. Dept. of agriculture. Index to Farmer's bulletins, nos. 1501–1750. Wash., D. C., Govt. print. off., 1941. 135 p.

*U. S. Dept. of agriculture. Index to publications of the U. S. Dept. of agriculture, by Mary A. Bradley. Wash., D. C., Govt. print. off., 1932–1937.
1901–1925; 2689p.
1926–1930; 694p.
1931–1935; 516p.

U. S. Dept. of agriculture. Index to Technical bulletins, 1–500, by Mabel G. Hunt. Wash., D. C., Govt. print. off., 1937. 249p.

U. S. Dept. of agriculture. Index to the Annual reports of the U. S. Dept. of agriculture, 1837–1893. (Publications division bulletin 1.) Wash., D. C., Govt. print. off., 1896 (reprint 1899). 252p.

U. S. Dept. of agriculture. Index to the Yearbooks of the Dept. of agriculture, 1894–1915. v. 1, 1894–1900; v. 2, 1901–1905; v. 3, 1906–1910; v. 4, 1911–1915. (Publications division bulletin 7, 9, 10.) Wash., D. C., Govt. print. off., 1902–1922. 196p; 166p; 146p; 178p.

U. S. Dept. of agriculture. List by titles of publications of the U. S. Dept. of agriculture from 1840 to June 1901, inclusive. (Publications division bulletin 6.) Wash., D. C., Govt. print. off., 1902. 216p.

U. S. Dept. of agriculture. List of publications of the agriculture dept., 1862–1902, with analytical index. (Bibliography of U. S. public documents, dept. lists 1.) Wash., D. C., Govt. print. off., 1904. 623p.

U. S. Dept. of agriculture. Synoptical index of the reports of the statistician, 1863–1894, by George F. Thompson. (Publications division bulletin 2.) Wash., D. C., Govt. print. off., 1897. 258p.

U. S. Library of congress. Legislative reference service. Digest of outstanding state legislation on agriculture, 1935–1939. (State law index, State law digest, report 4.) Wash., D. C., Govt. print. off., 1940.

U. S. Office of experiment stations. Experiment station record: general index. v. 1–12, 1889–1901; v. 13–25, 1901–1911; v. 26–40, 1912–1919; v. 41–50, 1919–1924; v. 51–60, 1924–1929; v. 61–70, 1929–1934. Wash., D. C., Govt. print. off., 1903–1937. 671p; 1159p; 640p; 709p; 677p; 752p.

U. S. Plant industry bureau. Contents of an index to the Bulletins of the Bureau of plant industry, nos. 1–100 inclusive. (Bulletin 101.) Wash., D. C., Govt. print. off., 1907. 102p.

U. S. Plant quarantine bureau. Cumulative index to Service and regulatory announcements, nos. 1–117, 1914–1933. Wash., D. C., Govt. print. off., 1934. 68p.

Anatomy

American journal of anatomy. Philadelphia, Pa. Index, v. 1–18, 1901–1915.

Anatomical record. Baltimore, Md. Index, v. 1–10, 1906–1916.

Anthropology

American anthropological association. General index, American anthropologist, Current anthropological literature, and Memoirs of the A.A.S., 1888–1928, 1929–1938. Menasha, Wisconsin.

American journal of physical anthropology. Index, v. 1–12, 1918–1937. Compiled by W. Montague Cobb, under the direction of Ales Hrdlicka. Mexico, D. F., 1941.

Antiques

*Antiques; a monthly magazine for collectors and amateurs. N.Y. Cumulative index, v. 1–30, 1922–1936.

Antiquities

See also **Archaeology**.

American antiquarian society. Proceedings. Worcester, Mass. Contents of proceedings, 1880–1903; partial index to proceedings, 1812–1880.

Society for the preservation of New England antiquities. Old-time New England. Boston. Index, v. 1–10, 1910–1919.

Archaeology

American journal of archaeology. Concord, N. H. Index, v. 1–10, 1895–1896; ser 2, v. 1–10, 1897–1906.

California University. Publications in American archaeology and ethnology. Authors and title index . . . v. 1-26, 1903-1929. Berkeley, University of California press, 1929. 16p.

Gomme, George Laurence and others. Index to archaeological papers, 1665-1890. Congress of archaeological societies in union with the Society of antiquaries. London, Constable, 1907. 8v.

Gomme, George Laurence and others. Index to archaeological papers, 1891-1910. Congress of archaeological societies in union with the Society of antiquaries. London, Constable, 1892-1914. 20v.

Records of the past. Wash., D. C. Index, v. 1-12, 1902-1913.

Architecture

American architect and the architectural review. Boston. Decennial index of phot-lithographic and other illustrations published in the American architect and building news, 1876-1885.

American institute of architects. Proceedings. Wash., D. C. Index, v. 1-10, 1867-1876.

Architectural record. N. Y. Index, v. 1-20, 1891-1906.

Index of literature from the publications of architectural societies . . . In American institute of architects quarterly bulletin. Wash., D. C., v. 1-13, 1900-1912. Continued as Journal of American institute of architects, v. 1, 1913-date.

Art

See also **Antiquities; Museums; Pictures,** etc.

*Art index, 1929-date. A cumulative author and subject index to a selected list of fine arts periodicals and museum bulletins. N. Y., Wilson, 1930-date.

School arts magazine. Worcester, Mass. Index, v. 1-11, 1901-1913.

Artists

Gage, Thomas Hovey. An artist's index to Stauffer's "American engravers," by Thomas Hovey Gage. Worcester, Mass., American antiquarian society, 1921. 49p. (Reprint from Proceedings of the American antiquarian society, October, 1920.)

Index of twentieth century artists. N. Y. Index, 1, 2, 3, 1933-1937. (In v. 3, no. 11-12.)

*Mallett, Daniel T. Index of artists (international-biographical). N. Y., Bowker, 1935. 493p.
Supplement, 1940. 319p.

Smith, Ralph C. Biographical index of American artists. Baltimore, Williams and Wilkins, 1930. 102p.

Astronomy

See also **Astrophysics.**

Astronomical society of the Pacific. Publications. San Francisco. Index, v. 1-25, 1889-1913.

Astronomy and astro-physics. Northfield, Minn. Index, v. 1–13, 1882–1894.

Harvard university. Observatory. Bulletin. Cambridge, Mass. Index, 751–800, 801–849 (as bulletin 850), 851–875.

Harvard university. Observatory. Harvard annals. Cambridge, Mass. Index, v. 1–78, 1855–1917.

Astrophysics

Astronomy and astro-physics, see **Astronomy.**

Astrophysical journal. Chicago. General index by authors and subjects, v. 1–25, 1895–1907; v. 26–50, 1908–1919; v. 51–75, 1920–1932.

Authors

Crooks, Muriel Augusta. Essays on modern authors; an index for high school use. Chicago, A.L.A., 1935. 31p. planographed.

Grismer, Raymond L. A reference index to 12,000 Spanish-American authors. (ser 3, no. 1.) N. Y., Wilson, 1939. 150p.

*Moulton, Charles Wells. Library of literary criticism of English and American authors. Buffalo, Moulton pub. co., 1901–1905. (Index in v. 8, p. 515–707.)

Bacteriology

Abstracts of bacteriology, 1917–1925. Baltimore, Society of American bacteriologists, 1917–1925. (Indexes) Merged with Botanical abstracts to form Biological abstracts.

Journal of bacteriology. Baltimore, Md. Index, authors and subjects, v. 1–30, 1916–1930.

Ballads

Holmes, Thomas James and George W. Thayer. English ballads and songs. Cleveland, O., Cleveland public library, 1931. 85p.

Hustvedt, Sigurd Barnhard. Ballad books and ballad men. Cambridge, Mass., Harvard univ. press, 1930. 376p. (The Gruntvig-Child index of English and Scottish popular ballads, p. 305–335.)

Hustvedt, Sigurd Barnhard. A melodic index of Child's ballad tunes. (Publications of University of California at Los Angeles in language and literature, v. 1, no. 2.) Berkeley, Calif., University of California press, 1936. 78p.

London. Stationers' company. An analytical index to the ballad-entries (1557–1709) in the registers of the Company of stationers of London, compiled by Hyder E. Rollins. Chapel Hill, N. C., University of North Carolina press, 1924. 324p. (Also *in* Studies in philology, 21: 1–324, Jan. 1924.)

Bibliography

American library annual, 1911–1912, 1917–1918, v. 1–7. N. Y., Bowker, 1912–1918.

*The Bibliographic index, a cumulative bibliography of bibliographies. N. Y., Wilson, 1938–date. Quarterly.

Bibliographical society of America. Index to the publications of the Bibliographical society of America and the Bibliographical society of Chicago, 1899–1931. Chicago, University of Chicago press, 1931. 43p. (Covers Yearbook of the Bibliographical society of Chicago, 1899/1900 to 1902/3; the Bulletin of Bibliographical society of America, v. 1–4, 1907/09–1912, and its Papers, v. 1–3, Proceedings and papers, v. 1–25, 1904/06–1931.)

Cole, George Watson, ed. Index to bibliographical papers published by the Bibliographical society and the Library association, London, 1877–1932. Chicago, Univ. of Chicago press, 1933. 262p.

Harvard university. Library. Index of reference lists and special bibliographies included in periodicals and other publications of recent date (1894-1891) by William C. Lane. Cambridge, Mass., Harvard univ. press, 1885–1891. (Library of Harvard university: Bibliographical contributions nos. 20, 24, 29, 40. Harvard university bulletins no. 32, 36, 39, 48.)

Nachtmann, Alice Newman. Index to subject bibliographies in library bulletins to Dec. 31, 1897. (N. Y. state library bulletin, bibliography 14.) Albany, N. Y., State library, 1898. p. 367–428.

Northup, Clark S. Register of bibliographies of the English language and literature. New Haven, Conn., Yale university press, 1925. 507p.

Providence. Public library. Index to reference lists published by libraries, 1907–1908, 1909, 1910–1938. *In* Bulletin of bibliography 5:125–126, 149–152, October 1908–Jan. 1909; 5:74–77, April 1901 and each January number, 1911–1938.

Providence. Public library. Index to reference lists published in library bulletins, October 1901–December 1906. (Bulletin of bibliography pamphlet 16.) Boston, Boston book co., 1907. 31p. (Reprinted from Bulletin of bibliography, Jan.–April 1907.)

Providence. Public library. Quarterly index to reference lists in other libraries. *In* Monthly bulletin of the Providence public library, v. 1–5. 1895–1899. *Cf* Bulletin of bibliography v. 2–4, 1899–1906.

Van Patten, Nathan. An index to bibliographies and bibliographical contributions relating to the work of American and British authors, 1923–1932. Stanford uni., Calif., Stanford university press, 1934. 324p.

Biography

See also **Artists; Authors; Botanists,** etc.

American biography, a new cyclopedia. Index, v. 1–50. Published under the direction of the American historical society, N. Y., 1932. 343p.

Cole, Eva Alice. Check list of biographical directories and general catalogues of American colleges. *In* N. Y. Genealogical and biographical record 46:51–57, 1915.

Current biography, who's news and why. N. Y., Wilson, 1940–date. Monthly, with cumulative index to preceding issues.

*Dictionary of American biography. N. Y., Scribners, 1937. 613p. (Index volume.)

*Dictionary of national biography... with an index covering the years 1901–1930 in one alphabetical series. Oxford, 1937.

Harvard university. Harvard-Yenching institute. Index to 33 collections of Ch'ing dynasty biographies. (Sinological series 9.) Cambridge, Mass., Harvard university press, 1933. 413p.

*Hefling, Helen and Jessie W. Dyde. Index to contemporary biography and criticism. 2d ed. Boston, Faxon, 1934. 229p.

Ireland, Norma Olin. Historical biographies. Phil., McKinley pub. co., 1933. 108p.

*Logasa, Hannah. Biography in collections; suitable for junior and senior high schools. 3d ed., rev. and enl. N. Y., Wilson, 1940. 152p.

*National cyclopedia of American biography: indexes — personal and topical indexes to the published volumes. N. Y., J. T. White and co., 1935. 254p.

O'Neill, Edward H. Biography by Americans, 1658–1936, a subject bibliography. Philadelphia, University of Pennsylvania press, 1939. 465p.

Phillips, Lawrence Barnett. Dictionary of biographical reference, containing over 100,000 names; together with a classified index of the biographical literature of Europe and America. new ed., rev., corrected and augmented with supplement to date by Frank Weitenkampf. London, Low; Philadelphia, Gebbie, 1889. 1038p.

Riches, Phyllis. Analytical bibliography of universal collected biography, comprising books published in the English tongue in Great Britain and Ireland, American and British dominions. London, Library association; N. Y., Wilson, 1934. 709p.

Sears, Minnie Earl and Marian Shaw. Essay and general literature index, *see* **Essays.**

Sears, Minnie Earl and others. Standard catalog for public libraries (Analytical index), *see* **Books.**

Smith, Theodore C. General index to the American statesman series. Boston, Houghton Mifflin, 1917. v. 40. 455p.

White's conspectus, *see* National Cyclopedia of American biography.

Wilson, Florence H. Bibliography of American biography. Phil., McKinley publishing co., 1930. 64p.

Biology

See also **Bacteriology; Botany; Zoology.**

Biological abstracts... Phil., Union of American biological societies 1926–date. (December no. is annual index.)

Biological bulletin. Lancaster, Pa. Index to v. 1–60, including v. 1 and 3 of the Zoological bulletin, 1898–1931.

Biological society of Washington. Proceedings. Wash., D. C. Author Index to Proceedings, v. 1–35, 1881–1922.

Johns Hopkins university. Biological laboratory. Studies. Baltimore, Md. Index, v. 1–5, 1887–1893.

Journal of biological chemistry, *see* **Chemistry.**

Birds
See **Ornithology.**

Blind
American association of instructors of the blind. Proceedings. Pittsburgh, Pa. Index, 1872–1920, 1922–1930.

Outlook for the blind. N. Y., American foundation for the blind. Index, v. 1–25, 1907–1931.

Book Collecting
The Colophon. N. Y. Index, v. 1, 2, 3, 4, 5, 1930–1935.

Book Reviews
See also special subjects, i.e. **Technology.**

*Book review digest. Index, 1917–1921 (in 1921); 1922–1926 (in 1926); 1927–1931 (in 1931); 1932–1936 (in 1936). N. Y., Wilson co.

Booklist. Chicago, American library association. Subject index, v. 1–6, Jan. 1905–June 1910.

New York Herald Tribune. Books index. (Published twice a year.)

Review index; a quarterly guide to professional reviews for college and reference libraries. Edited by Louis Kaplan and Clarence S. Paine. v. 1, 1940–date. Chicago, Follett book co., 1940–date.

Books
See also **Incunabula; Pamphlets; Special Collections,** etc.

Astor library, N. Y. Supplement to the Astor library catalogue with an alphabetical index of subjects in all the volumes. N. Y., Craighead press, 1866. 605p.

British museum. Subject index of the modern books added to the library. N. Y., Oxford univ. press.
1881–1900 (3v.)
1901–1905
1906–1910
1911–1915
1916–1920
1921–1925 (without books relating to the European war)
1926–1930
1931–1935 (2v.)

Cumulative book index. N. Y., Wilson. (Continues U. S. Catalog.)

English catalogue of books ... issued in the United Kingdom, being a continuation of the "London" and "British" catalogues ... 1835–date. London, Publishers' circular, 1837–date.

English catalogue of books published 1801–1930. London, S. Low, 1864–1905; London, Low 1912–1931. 13v. (Index, v. 1–4 only.)

London library. Subject index of the London library, by C. T. Hagberg Wright. London, 1908–1923. 2v.

Peddie, Robert Alexander. Subject index of books published up to and including 1880; A-Z. London, Grafton and co. 745p.

Proctor, Robert. An index to the early printed books in the British museum. Pt. 2., 1501–1520. Section 1, Germany. London, K. Paul, 1903. 273p.

Section 2, 1501–1520. Sect. 2, Italy; sect. 3, Switzerland and eastern Europe, by Frank Isaac. London, Quaritch, 1938. 286p.

Supplements, 1898–1902. London, 1900–1903, 5pts.

*Sears, Minnie Earl and others. Standard catalog for public libraries. N. Y., Wilson, 1940. (Analytical index, p. 1475–2192.)

Sonneschein, William Swan. The best books. 3d ed. N. Y. Putnam, 1935. (Part VI, Index, p. 3385–3760.)

Subscription books bulletin. Chicago, A.L.A. Index, v. 1–4, 1930–1933 (Oct. 1933, p. 51–64); v. 5–8, Jan. 1934–Oct. 1937 (Oct. 1937, p. 61–64); v. 9, no. 1–v. 11, no. 4 (Oct. 1940, p. 54–56).

U. S. Catalog. N. Y., Wilson, 1898–date. (Continued by Cumulative book index.)

Books — Prices

American book prices current. Index to American book prices current, 1916–1922, compiled by Philip Sanford Goulding, and Helen Plummer Goulding. N. Y., Dutton, 1925. 1379p.

American book prices current. A priced index, 1923–1932. Compiled by Eugenia Wallace and Lucie E. Wallace. N. Y., Bowker, 1936. 1007p.

American book prices current. Index to American book prices current, 1933–1940, edited by Edward Lazare. N. Y., Bowker, 1941. 499p.

Book-auction records. London, Henry Stevens
General index, 1902–1912, v. 1–9
2d general index, 1912–1923, v. 10–20
3d general index, 1924–1933, v. 21–30
Book prices current. London, Stock
Index to the first decade, 1887–1896
Index to the 2d decade, 1897–1906
Index to the 3d decade, 1907–1916

Trade prices current of American first editions, 1936–1939. N. Y., Bowker, 1939. 229p.

Botanists

Britten, James and George S. Boulger, compilers. Biographical index of deceased British and Irish botanists. 2d ed. rev. London, Taylor and Francis, 1931. 342p.

Botany

See also **Horticulture.**

Addisonia. N. Y. Alphabetical index to v. 6–10, 1922–1925 (in v. 10, 1925, p. 73–74); Taxonomic index to v. 6–10, 1922–1925 (in v. 10, 1925, p. 69–71); Alphabetical index to v. 11–15, 1926–1930 (in v. 15, 1930, p. 70–71); Taxonomic index to v. 11–15, 1926–1930 (in v. 15, p. 68–69).

AN INDEX TO INDEXES 11

Botanical abstracts; cumulated author and subject index for v. 1–10, Sept. 1918–Feb. 1922. Baltimore, Md., Williams and Wilkins, 1924. 418p. (Merged with Abstracts of bacteriology to form Biological abstracts.)

Botanical gazette. Crawfordsville, Ind. Index, v. 1–10, 1875–1885.

Botanical review, interpreting botanical progress. Lancaster, Pa. Indices, v. 1–5, 1935–1939.

Boyce Thompson institute for plant research, inc. Contributions. Yonkers, N. Y. Index to v. 1–10, 1925–1939, compiled by Zeliette Troy. (Published as v. 11, no. 1 pt. 2.)

Bryologist. Brooklyn, N. Y. Index, v. 1–10, 1898–1907.

Journal of mycology. Columbus, O. Index, v. 1–10, 1885–1908.

Mycologia. Lancaster, Pa. (Continues Journal of mycology.) Index, v. 1–24, 1909–1932.

N. Y. Botanical gardens. Journal. N. Y. Index to v. 1–15, 1900–1914. v. 16–30, 1915–1929.

Phytopathology. Lancaster, Pa., American phytopathological soc. Thirty year index, v. 1–30, 1911–1940.

Torrey botanical club. Bulletin. N. Y. Index, v. 1–16, 1870–1889.

Business and Commerce

See also **Directories; Economics; Salesmanship; Tariff,** etc.

American management association. The management index; a subject index to the publications of the A.M.A. Jan. 1923 to Jan. 1932. N. Y., A.M.A., 1932. 92p.

Davenport, Donald Hills and Frances V. Scott. An index to business indices. Chicago, Business publications, inc., 1937. 187p.

Federal reserve bulletin. Wash., D. C., Fed. reserve board. Index-digest, v. 1–6 inclusive, 1914–1920, by Charles S. Hamlin.

*Fortune. N. Y., Time-Fortune corporation. Index, v. 1–16, 1930–1937 (*see also* Vocational index to Fortune, under **Vocations.**)

Harvard business reports. Chicago, Ill. Cumulative index, v. 1–10, 1925–1932.

Harvard business review. Cambridge, Mass. Cumulative index, v. 1–15, 1922–1937.

Merchants' magazine and commercial review. N. Y. Index, v. 1–10, 1839–1844.

National foreign trade council. A topical index of addresses on foreign trade, delivered before the annual foreign trade conventions 1914–1929. N. Y., Council, India House, 1930. 16p.

National retail dry goods association. Controller's congress. N. Y. Index of convention reports of the controllers' congress (1st through 19th inclusive). *In* its Annual convention . . . Report . . . v. 20, 1939, p. 169–191.

Special libraries association. Guides to business facts and figures. An indexed and descriptive list emphasizing the less known business reference sources. N. Y., The Assoc., 1937. 59p.

U. S. Bureau of foreign and domestic commerce. Index to the Consular reports, nos. 1–239 (v. 1–63, Oct. 1880–August 1900). Wash., D. C., Govt. print. off., 1887–1901.

U. S. Bureau of foreign commerce. List of available publications issued, corrected to Jan. 1, 1940. Wash., D. C., Govt. print. off., 1940. 30p.

U. S. Federal trade commission. Index-digest of v. 1, 2, 3 of Decisions of the Federal trade commission with annotations of federal cases, March 16, 1915 to June 30, 1921. Wash., D. C., Govt. print. off., 1922. 233p.

U. S. Interstate commerce commission. Reports. Decisions. Consolidated index to the Reported decisions of the I. C. C., v. 1–85 inclusive (except finance and valuation decisions); compiled by Edwin C. Blanchard and Fred W. Heid. Wash., D. C., Capital traffic service bureau, 1925. 292p.

Business Education

Business education index, 1940; an author and subject index of business education articles compiled from a selected list of periodicals and yearbooks published during the year 1940. Sponsored by Delta Pi Epsilon. edited by Eugene H. Hughes. N. Y., Business education world, 1941. 36p.

Selby, Paul Owen, comp. Index to collegiate business education; a comprehensive bibliography, covering the years 1929–1938 inclusive. Kirksville, Mo., Research press, 1939. 39p.

Selby, Paul Owen, comp. Index to the teaching of general business, 1929–1938: junior business training, senior business training, introduction to business, consumer-business economics. Kirksville, Mo., Research press, 1939. 48p.

Business Law

Selby, Paul Owen, comp. Index to the teaching of business law, 1929–1939. Kirksville, Mo., Research press, 1939. 71p.

California — History

Grizzly bear. Los Angeles, Calif. Index, v. 1–20, 1907–1917.

Historical society of Southern California. Publications. Los Angeles, Calif. Index, v. 1–11, 1884–1920.

Canada

Canadian periodical index, 1938–date. A cumulation of the quarterly indexes published in the Ontario library review, compiled by the Circulation dept. of the University of Toronto library. Toronto, Canada, Public libraries br., Ontario dept. of education, 1939. (Continued by quarterly indexes in Ontario library review. Serves as a continuation with an interval of some 5 years, of the earlier Canadian index.)

Canadian periodical index, 1st annual cumulation, 1931. Windsor, Ontario public library, 1932. (Continued 1932 by quarterly multigraphed numbers; discontinued 1932, followed by above, 1938.)

Catholics

American Catholic historical society of Philadelphia. Records. Index, v. 1–31, 1884–1920.

American Catholic quarterly review. Philadelphia. Index, v. 1–25, Ja. 1876–Oct. 1900.

Brown, Stephen James Meredith. International index of Catholic biographies (Catholic bibliographical series) 2d ed. rev. & enl. London, Burns, 1935. 285p.

*Catholic encyclopedia. N. Y. Catholic ency. pr. 1907–1922 (Index in v. 16).

The Catholic historical review. Wash., D. C. General index to v. 1–20, April 1915/Jan. 1935, by Rev. Harold J. Bolton.

Catholic library world, *see* **Library Science.**

Catholic periodical index, 1930–date; a guide to Catholic magazines. Published for the library section of the National Catholic education association by H. W. Wilson co. Scranton, Pa., Natl. Catholic educ. assoc., 1931/32–date (Quarterly since 1940).

Catholic world. N. Y. Index, v. 1–63, 1865–1896.

Guide to Catholic literature, 1888–1940. Detroit, Romig, 1940. 1240p.

Index librorum prohibitorum. Index of prohibited books, revised and published by order of His Holiness Pope Pius XI. new ed. Vatican city, Vatican polyglot press, 1930. 563p.

Willging, Eugene Paul. The index to American Catholic pamphlets. Saint Paul, Minn., Catholic library service, 1937. 128p.

Supplements, 1, 2, 3 (Cumulative and later supplement underway).

Census

U. S. Bureau of census. Index of data tabulated from the 1930 census of population, including unemployment. Wash., D. C., Govt. print. off., 1940. 47p.

U. S. Bureau of census. Topical index of population census reports, 1900–1930. Wash., D. C., Govt. print. off., 1934. 76p.

Ceramics

American ceramic society. Ceramic abstracts, 1922–date. Easton, Pa., American ceramic society, 1922–date. (Indexes.)

American ceramic society. Transactions. Easton, Pa. Collective index, compiled and edited by E. J. Crane and E. Hockett, v. 1–19, 1889–1917.

Ceramic industry. Chicago, Ill. Index to v. 1–3, 1923–1924.

Solon, Louis Marc Emmanuel. Ceramic literature, an analytical index to the works published in all languages on the history and technology of the ceramic art, etc. London, Griffin, 1910. 660p.

Charities

See **Social Service.**

Chemical Engineering

American institute of chemical engineers. Transactions. N. Y. Index to v. 1–15, 1908–1922, compiled by Harold F. Whittaker.

Chemistry

See also **Agricultural Chemistry; Chemical Engineering; Electrochemistry.**

American chemical journal, *see* American chemical society. Journal.

*American chemical society. Chemical abstracts. Easton, Pa. Decennial indexes: v. 1–10, 1907–1916; v. 11–20, 1917–1926; v. 21–30, 1927–1936.

American chemical society. Journal. Easton, Pa. v. 1–10, 1879–1888; v. 11–20, 1889–1898; v. 21–50, 1899–1913.

American institute of chemical engineers. Transactions. N. Y. Index, v. 1–15, 1908–1922; v. 16–30, 1923–1941.

American leather chemists association. Journal. Easton, Pa. 10 year indexes: v. 1–10, 1906–1915; v. 11–20, 1916–1925.

American society for testing materials. Index to the literature on spectrochemical analysis, 1920–1937, by William F. Meggers and Bourdon F. Scribner; publications sponsored by Com. E–2 on spectographic analysis of the society. The society, 1939. 59p.

Chemical reviews. Baltimore, American chemical society. Author index, v. 1–10, 1924–1931, and Subject index, v. 1–10, 1924–1931 (In v. 10, 1931, p. 495–506); v. 11–20, 1932–1937.

Journal of biological chemistry. Baltimore, Md.
Index, v. 1– 25, 1905–1916
26– 50, 1916–1922
51– 75, 1922–1928
76–100, 1928–1933
101–125, 1933–1938

Mellor, Joseph W. Comprehensive treatise on inorganic and theoretical chemistry. N. Y., Longmans, Green, 1922–1927. 16v. (Index.)

Rubber chemistry and technology. Easton, Pa., American chemical, society, Rubber division. Index, v. 1–10, 1928–1937.

Thorpe, Jocelyn Field. Dictionary of applied chemistry. N. Y., Longmans, Green, 1927. (Index, v. 7, p. 611–765.) Supplement index, v. 3, p. 101–166.

Worden, Edward C. Chemical patents index, *see* **Patents.**

Children

Child health bulletin. N. Y., American child health association. Cumulative index, Mar. 1925 through Dec. 1927.

Parents' magazine. Index to authoritative articles on every child rearing problem. Jamaica, N. Y., Parents' magazine, 1934.

Children's Literature

See also **Children's Plays; Children's Poetry; Encyclopedias; Fairy Tales; Readers.**

The Horn book. Boston, Women's educational and industrial union. Index, from v. 1, no. 1, Oct. 1924 through v. 5, no. 4, Nov. 1929.

Miller, Olive Beaupré, ed. My bookhouse. Chicago, Bookhouse for children, 1921. The Latchkey, v. 6. 320p.

Ohr, Elizabeth, comp. Stories and poems for opening exercises, an index. Chicago, A.L.A., 1927. 46p.

Rue, Eloise. Subject index to books for intermediate grades, see **Readers.**

Rue, Eloise. Subject index to readers, see **Readers.**

*Saint Nicholas. N. Y., Wilson co. Index, v. 1-45, 1873-1918, by A. L. Guthrie.

Salisbury, Grace E. and M. E. Beckwith. Index to short stories. Evanston, Ill., Row, Peterson & co. 1907. 118p.

Wead, Katherine H. List of series and sequels for juvenile readers, see **Series, Books in.**

Wurzburg, Dorothy A., comp. Children's short story index for special holidays. Boston, Faxon, 1928. 116p.

Wurzburg, Dorothy A. East, West, North and South in children's books. Boston, Faxon, 1939. 158p.

Young wings. N. Y., Junior literary guild. Index, v. 1-10, 1929-1939, compiled by Carolyn F. Ulrich.

Children's Plays

A.L.A. Board on library service to children and young people. Subcommittee. Subject index to children's plays. Chicago, A.L.A., 1940. 277p.

Hazeltine, Alice I. Plays for children, an annotated index. 2d ed. rev. Chicago, A.L.A., 1921. 116p.

Hyatt, Aeola L. Index to children's plays. 3d ed. rev. and enl. Chicago, A.L.A., 1931. 214p.

Paulmier, Hilah. Index to holiday plays for schools. N. Y., Wilson, 1936. 59p.

Children's Poetry

Brewton, J. E. Index to children's poetry. N. Y., Wilson, 1941. (in press.)

McPherson, Maud R. Children's poetry index. Boston, Faxon, 1938. 453p.

Children's Songs

Cushing, Helen Grant. Children's song index. N. Y., Wilson, 1936. 789p.

Quigley, Marjory C. Index to kindergarten songs, including singing games. Chicago, A.L.A., 1914. 286p.

Civil Engineering

American society of civil engineers. Transactions. N. Y. Index, v. 1-83, 1867-1920.

Classical Literature
Classical journal. Cedar Rapids, Iowa. General index, v. 1–25, 1905–1930, by Franklin H. Potter.

Classical weekly. N. Y., Classical association of the Atlantic states. Index, v. 1–16, 1907–1923, by Charles Knapp (issued as Pt. 2 of Classical weekly), v. 17, no. 9–23, Dec. 10, 1923–April 21, 1924.

Club Programs
Henry, Elizabeth G. Helps for club program makers. Chicago, A.L.A., 1935. 86p.

Coins
See **Numismatics.**

College Athletics
National collegiate athletic association. Proceedings. N. Y. Index, 1906–1934.

Colonization
African repository. Wash., D. C., American colonization society. Index, v. 1–10, 1825–1834.

American colonization society. Annual report. Wash., D. C. Index, v. 1–18, 1818–1835.

Commerce
See **Business and Commerce.**

Copyrights
U. S. Copyright office. Catalog of copyright entries. Wash., D. C., Govt. print. off., 1891–date. (Volume indexes.)

Costume
Hiler, Hilaire and Meyer Hiler. Bibliography of costume. N. Y., Wilson, 1939. 911p.

*Monro, Isabel and Dorothy E. Cook. Costume index. N. Y., Wilson, 1937. 338p.

Crafts
See **Handicrafts.**

Crime and Criminals
Culver, Dorothy, comp. Author index to A Guide to material on crime and criminal justice. N. Y., Wilson, 1934. 32p.

Journal of criminal law and criminology. Chicago, American institute of criminal law and criminology. Index, v. 1–24, 1910–1934.

U. S. Federal bureau of investigation. Uniform crime reports. . . . Ten year index, 1930–1939, v. 1–10. Wash., D. C., Govt. print. off., 1941.

Wire, G. E. Index of celebrated cases, crimes, criminals, detectives, escapes, homicides, mysteries, swindles, trials, etc. described in general books (not in volumes specifically devoted to the particular case or person). Journal of criminal law, 21:339-63, Nov. 1930. Chicago, American institute of criminal law and criminology.

Dances
See **Games and Dances.**

Dates
American library annual, *see* **Bibliography.**

Annual library index, *see* **Literature.**

Annual literary index, *see* **Literature.**

Little, Charles E. Cyclopedia of classified dates with exhaustive index. N. Y., Funk, 1900. 1454p.

New York Times index, *see* **Newspapers.**

Debate
Johnsen, Julia E. Debate index supplement. (Reference shelf, v. 14, no. 9.) N. Y., Wilson, 1941. 90p.

Miller, Marion Mills. Great debates in American history. N. Y., Current literature publishing co., 1913. v. 14, p. 405-501.

*Phelps, Edith May, ed. Debate index. (Reference shelf, v. 12, no. 9.) N. Y., Wilson, 1939. 130p.

Pittsburgh. Carnegie Library. Debate index. 3d ed. Pittsburgh, Carnegie library, 1919. 116p.

Dentistry
Black, Arthur D. Index of the periodical dental literature published in the English language. Buffalo, N. Y., Dental index bureau, 1839-date.

N. Y. Academy of medicine. Dental bibliography, a reference index to the literature of dental science . . . compiled by Bernard W. Weinberger, N. Y., First district dental society, state of N. Y., 1929. 183p.

Dialogs
Ireland, Norma Olin and David E. Ireland. Index to monologs and dialogs, *see* **Monologs.**

Diplomatic Service
See **U. S. Foreign Relations.**

Directories
Cannons, Harvey George T. Classified guide to 1700 annuals, directories, calendars and yearbooks. N. Y., Wilson, 1923. 196p.

Manley, Marian C., comp. Business directories: a key to their use. Newark, N. J., The public library, 1934. 63p.

Morley, Linda H. and Adelaide C. Knight. Mailing list directory. A classified index to trade directories. N. Y., McGraw-Hill, 1924. 727p.

Special libraries association. Business and trade directories. A classified guide to the sources of business terminology and definitions. N. Y., Special libraries assoc., 1934. 39p.

Dissertations

See also **Universities and Colleges.**

Gilchrist, Donald B., ed. Doctoral dissertations accepted by American universities. N. Y., Wilson, 1933–date.

no. 1, 1933–1934
no. 2, 1934–1935
no. 3, 1935–1936
no. 4, 1936–1937
no. 5, 1937–1938
no. 6, 1938–1939
no. 7, 1939–1940

Knower, Franklin H. Graduate theses; an index of graduate work in the field of speech, see **Speech.**

Palfrey, Thomas A. and Henry E. Coleman, Jr. Guide to bibliographies of theses — United States and Canada. 2d ed. N. Y., Wilson, 1940. 54p. planographed.

U. S. Library of Congress. Catalog division. List of American dissertations printed . . . 1912–date (annual). Wash., D. C., Govt. print. off., 1912–date.

Documents

See **Government Documents.**

Drama

See also **Children's Plays; Theatre.**

Baker, Blanch M., comp. Dramatic bibliography. N. Y., Wilson, 1932. (Analytical subject index, p. 283–320.) 320p.

Dramatic index for 1909–date, covering articles and illustrations concerning the stage . . . Boston, Faxon, 1910–date. (Issued separately and also as Part 2 of Annual magazine subject index, 1909–date. Kept up-to-date by indexes in the Bulletin of Bibliography.)

Dramatist, a journal of dramatic technology. Easton, Pa. Index, v. 1–14, 1909–1923.

*Firkins, Ida Ten Eyck. Index to plays, 1800–1926. N. Y., Wilson, 1927. 307p.

Supplement, 1927–1935. N. Y., Wilson, 1935. 140p.

*Logasa, Hannah and Winifred Ver Nooy. Index to one-act plays, 1924–1932. Boston, Faxon, 1932. 2v. 327p; 432p.

2d supplement, 1932–1940. Boston, Faxon, 1941. (xv+ 71.)

Pence, James Harry. The magazine and the drama, an index. N. Y., Dunlap society, 1896. 190p.

Sears, Minnie Earl and others. Standard catalog for public libraries (analytical index), see **Books.**

Silk, Agnes K. and Clara E. Fanning. Index to dramatic readings, see **Readings and Recitations.**

Smith, Milton Myers. Guide to play selection; a descriptive index of full length and short plays for production by schools, colleges and little theatres. N. Y., Appleton, 1934. 174p.

Economics

See also **Business and Commerce; Labor**, etc.

American economic association. Publications. N. Y. Index, 1886–1910. (*In* American economic review, v. 7, no. 4.)

Chase economic bulletin. N. Y., Chase national bank. Index, v. 1–12, inclusive, 1920–1932.

Hasse, Adelaide R. Index of economic material in documents of the states of the United States. Wash., D. C., Carnegie institute, 1907–1922. 13v. in 16.

Journal of farm economics, *see* **Agriculture.**

Education

See also **Business Education; Dissertations; Humanities; Units of Work; Universities and Colleges; Vocations.**

American council on education. Studies . . . series 3, Financial advisory service. Wash., D. C. Index, v. 1–4, nos. 1–8, 1935–1940.

American journal of education. Hartford, Conn. Index, v. 1–31, 1855–1881.

Education. Boston. Index, v. 1–25, 1880–1905.

Education abstracts (formerly Educational abstracts). Fulton, Mo. v. 1–5, 1936–1940.

*Education index, 1929–date. N. Y., Wilson, 1929–date.

Educational review. N. Y. Analytical index to v. 1–25, Jan. 1891–May 1903, edited by C. Nelson; analytical index to v. 26–50, June 1903–Dec. 1915, edited by Nicholas Murray Butler.

High points in the work of the high schools of N. Y. city. N. Y. Index, v. 1–18, 1919–1936.

Kindergarten-primary magazine. Chicago. Index, v. 1–15, 1888–1902.

Loyola educational index; a reader's guide to education and psychology. Chicago, Loyola university press, v. 1, 1928 (continued by Educational index).

Monroe, Walter Scott and Louis Shores. Bibliographies and summaries in education to July 1935. N. Y., Wilson, 1936. 470p.

National education association of U. S. Index by authors, titles and subjects to the publications of the N.E.A. for its first 50 years, 1857–1906. Comp. by Martha Furber Nelson. Winona, Miss., The Association. 211p.

North central association quarterly. Ann Arbor, Mich. 10-volume index, 1926–1936. (In v. 11, 1936/37.)

Pennsylvania school journal. Harrisburg, Pa. Pa. state education assoc. Index, v. 1–16, 1852–1868.

School review. Chicago. Index, v. 1–10, 1893–1902.

Selected references in education, reprinted from the School review and the Elementary school journal from January to December. (Supplementary educ. monographs.) Chicago, University of Chicago press, 1933–date. Author index.

U. S. Office of education. Bibliography of research studies in education. Wash., Govt. print. off., 1928–date. (Annual. Indexes of institutions, authors, subjects. Continues Monroe and Shores.) *In* Office of education Bulletin.

U. S. Office of education. Bulletins of the Bureau of education, 1906–1927, with index by author, title and subject, by Edith A. Wright and Mary S. Phillips. (Bulletin 1928, no. 17.) . . . Wash., D. C., Govt. print. off., 1928. 65p.

U. S. Office of education. Index to reports of Commissioner of education, 1867–1907. (Bulletin 1909, no. 7.) Wash., D. C., Govt. print. off., 1909. 103p.

*U. S. Office of education. List of publications of U.S. Bureau of education, 1867–1907. (Bulletin 1908, no. 2.) Wash., Govt. print. off., 1908. 55p.

*U. S. Office of education. List of publications of the Office of education, 1910–1936, including those of the former Federal board for vocational education for 1917–1933. (Bulletin 1937, no. 22.) Wash., D. C., Govt. print. off., 1938. 158p.

U. S. Office of education. Monthly record of educational publications. Wash., D. C., Govt. print. off., 1912–1933. (Preceeds Bibliography of research studies.)

Electrical Engineering

American institute of electrical engineers. Transactions. N. Y. Index, v. 1–29, 1884–1910; v. 30–40, 1911–1921; v. 41–57, 1922–1938.

Electricity

Electric journal (Electric club). Pittsburgh. Index (cumulative), v. 1–date in v. 2–10, 1904–date; v. 11–date in v. 12–15, 1914–date; v. 16–date in v. 17–20, 1919–date; v. 21–date in v. 22–25, 1924–date; v. 26–date in v. 27, 1929–date.

Electrical world. N. Y. Index, v. 1–28, 1883–1896; v. 29–52, 1897–1908.

National electric light association. Proceedings. N. Y. Index, v. 1–32, 1885–1909; v. 32–36, 1909–1913.

U. S. Patent office. Index of patents relating to electricity . . . *see* **Patents.**

Electrochemistry

Electrochemical society. Transactions. N. Y. General index, v. 1–20, 1902–1911; v. 21–40, 1912–1921; v. 41–60, 1922–1931.

Employment

U. S. Bureau of employment security. Employment service news. Cumulative index for September 1934 through December 1938. Wash., D. C., Govt. print. off., 1939. 35p.

AN INDEX TO INDEXES

Encyclopedias

Americana annual; an encyclopedia of current events. Chicago, Americana corporation. Cumulative index, 1923–1932, *in* 1933 annual; 1933–1940 *in* 1941 annual.

Britannica book of the year. Chicago. Ency. Britannica, 1938–date. (Index in each annual, with general index to articles in preceding annuals.)

Compton's pictured encyclopedia. rev. ed. Chicago, F. E. Compton co., 1941. Easy reference fact index (in back of each volume).

Encyclopedia Americana. N. Y., Ency. Americana corp., 1931–32. (Classified index, v. 30.)

*Encyclopedia Britannica. 14th ed. N. Y., Ency. Britannica co. (Index, in v. 24, p. 199–958.)

Lincoln library of essential information. Buffalo, N. Y., Frontier pr. co., 1940. Index.

Engineering

See also Chemical Engineering; Civil Engineering; Electrical Engineering; Mechanical Engineering; Municipal Engineering; Radio Engineering; Refrigeration.

American railway bridge and building association. Proceedings. Index of subjects, v. 1–30, 1891–1920.

American society for testing materials. Index to A.S.T.M. standards and tentative standards . . . as of Jan. 1, 1940. Phil., The society, 1940. 152p.

American society for testing materials. Proceedings. Phil., The society Indexes, v. 1–12, 1898–1912; v. 13–20, 1913–1920; v. 21–25, 1921–1925; v. 26–30, 1926–1930; v. 31–35, 1931–1935.

Black Hills engineer. South Dakota, Rapid City, South Dakota state school of mines. Chronological index; a list of the principal articles in the Pahasapa quarterly and the Black Hills engineer, 1911–1932, arranged by volume and number, in v. 20, 1932, p. 160–167; Author index, in v. 20, 1932, p. 167–175.

Cement and engineering news. Chicago. Index, v. 1–6, 1896–1899; v. 7–11, 1899–1901; v. 12–14, 1902–1903.

Cleveland engineering society. Journal. Cleveland, O. Index, v. 1–5, 1908–1913.

Engineering index, 1884–1905. N. Y., Engineering magazine, 1892–1906. Index, 1906–date. N. Y., Engineering magazine, 1907–1919; American society of mechanical engineers, 1920–date. (Supplemented by Engineering index service.)

Engineering news-record. N. Y., Engineering news pub. co. Index, v. 1–24, 1874–1890; v. 24–42, 1890–1899; v. 43–52, 1900–1904; v. 53–62, 1905–1909; v. 63–77, 1910–1917; v. 78–89, 1917–1922; v. 90–99, 1923–1927.

Engineering record, building record and sanitary engineer. N. Y. Index, v. 1–75, no. 13, Dec. 1877–March 1917.

Engineers' society of western Pennsylvania. Proceedings. Pittsburgh. Index, v. 1–20, 1880–1904.

Galloupe, Francis Ellis. Galloupe's general index to engineering periodicals. Boston, 1888–1893. 2v.

Iowa engineer. Ames, Ia. Index, v. 1–6, 1910–1906; v. 10–19, 1910–1919.

Iowa engineering society. Proceedings. Glenwood, Ia. Index, v. 1–38, 1889–1926 as Bulletin of the Associated state engineering societies, v. 2, no. 4, pt. 2.

Professional memoirs, corps of engineers, U. S. Army and Engineer dept. at large. Wash., D. C., Barracks. Index, v. 1–5, as v. 6, Supp. 2, 1909–1920.

Society for the promotion of engineering education. Proceedings. Lancaster, Pa. Index, v. 1–10, 1893–1902; v. 1–20, 1893–1912.

Society of motion picture engineers. Journal, *see* **Motion Pictures.**

Stevens indicator. Hoboken, N. J. Contents and index, v. 1–38, 1884–1921, *In* October 1921, p. 331–408.

U. S. Engineer dept. Index to the Reports of the chief engineers, U. S. Army (including the Reports of the Isthmian canal commissions, 1866–1917). Wash., D. C., Govt. print. off., 1915–1921. 3 v. v. 1, 1866–1912; v. 2, 1866–1912; v. 3, 1913–1917.

Western society of engineers. Journal. Chicago. Cumulative index, v. 1–20, 1896–1915; v. 21–31, 1916–1926.

Entomology

Bernice Pauahi Bishop museum. Pacific entomological survey. Index to P.E.S. publications (taxonomic papers only), *in* Bulletin 98, 113–114, 142, 1939. Honolulu, Hawaii, The museum.

Colcord, Mabel, comp. Index to the literature of American economic entomology. Melrose Highlands, Mass., American assoc. of econ. entomologists, 1915–date.

Index (1) 1905–1914   (5) 1930–1934
(2) 1915–1919
(3) 1920–1924
(4) 1924–1929

Currie, Rolla and Andrew N. Caudell. Index to Circulars 1–100 of the Bureau of entomology. (Circular 100.) Wash., D. C., 1911. 49p.

Psyche. Boston. Index, v. 1–10, 1920–1930.

U. S. Bureau of agricultural economics. The B.A.E. news, 1923–1926. Index to nos. 1–38, Jan. 16, 1923–Dec. 28, 1926. Wash., D. C., Govt. print. off., 1926.

U. S. Bureau of agricultural economics. General index to the seven volumes of Insect life, 1889–1895. Wash., D. C., Govt. print. off., 1897. 145p.

U. S. Dept. of agriculture. An index to Bulletins no. 1–30 (new series), 1896–1901 of the Division of entomology. Wash., D. C., Govt. print. off., 1902. 64p.

AN INDEX TO INDEXES

Essays
Brewer, David Josiah. World's best essays. St. Louis, Kaiser, 1900. 10v. (Index, v. 10.)

*Sears, Minnie Earl and Marian Shaw. Essay and general literature index, 1900/33 to date. N. Y., Wilson, 1934–date.
1900–1933   1934–1940 in preparation
1934–1936 supplement
1937 supplement

Ethics
Ethics. Chicago. Index, v. 1–41, 1890–1931.
International journal of ethics. Philadelphia. Index, v. 1–41, Oct. 1890–July 1931 (*In* v. 42, p. 45–112.)

Ethnology
California, University. Publications in American archaeology and ethnology, *see* **Archaeology**.

U. S. Bureau of ethnology. General index, annual reports of Bureau of American ethnology, v. 1–48, 1879–1931. Wash., D. C., Govt. print. off., 1933. (*In* 48th annual report of Bureau of American ethnology of Smithsonian institution, 1930–31, p. 25–1223.)

U. S. Bureau of ethnology. List of publications of American ethnology with index to authors and titles, revised to June 30, 1937. Wash., D. C., Govt. print. off., 1937.

European War, 1914-1918
British museum. Subject index of the books relating to the European war, 1914–1918, acquired by the Museum, 1914–1920. N. Y., Oxford univ. press, 1922. 196p.

Horne, Charles F., ed. Source records of the great war. Boston, Mass., Stuart Copley press, 1923. 7v. (Index, v. 7.)

Times, London. The Times diary and index of the war, 1914–1918. London, Hoder and Stoughton, 1921. 342p.

European War, 1939-
See also **Encyclopedias; Newspapers; Periodicals; Periodicals, General.**

War volume of Compton's pictured encyclopedia, an alphabetical record book of the European war. 6th ed. Chicago, F. E. Compton co., 1941. 126p. (Pronouncing index, p. 124–126.)

Fairy Tales
Eastman, Mary Huse. Index to fairy tales, myths and legends. 2d ed. rev. and enl. Boston, Faxon, 1926. 610p.

Supplement. Boston, Faxon, 1937. 566p.

Fiction
Baker, Ernest Albert and James Pachman. Guide to the best fiction, Engglish and American. New and enl. ed. N. Y., Macmillan, 1932. 634p. (Index to authors, titles, subjects, etc.)

Baker, Ernest Albert and James Pachman. Guide to historical fiction. N. Y., Macmillan, 1914. 566p. (Index to authors, titles, etc.)

Dixon, Zella Allen. Comprehensive index to universal prose fiction. N. Y., Dodd Mead, 1897. 421p.

Lenrow, Elbert. Reader's guide to prose fiction. N. Y., Appleton, 1940. 371p.

Lingenfelter, Mary R. Vocations in fiction, see **Vocations.**

Logasa, Hannah. Historical fiction. Phil., McKinley pub. co., 1930. 131p.

Nield, Jonathan. Guide to the best historical novels and tales. N. Y., Macmillan, 1929. 424p. (Includes index of authors, titles and subjects.)

Van Nostrand, Jeanne. Subject index to high school fiction. Chicago, A.L.A., 1938. 67p.

Fire Protection

National fire protection association. Publications. Boston. Index, 1897–1923.

Fisheries

American fisheries society. Transactions. Index, v. 1–58, 1872–1928.

U. S. Fisheries bureau. Analytical subject bibliography of the publications of the Bureau, 1871–1920 by Rose M. E. Macdonald. (Fisheries bureau document 899 and appendix 5 to the report of the U. S. Commissioner of Fisheries for 1920.) Wash., D. C., Govt. print. off., 1921. 306p.

Florida — History

Florida historical society. The quarterly periodical. Jacksonville, Fla. Index, v. 1–6, 1908–1928, v. 7–14, 1928–1936.

Folk Lore

American folk-lore society. Memoirs. Boston. Index, v. 1–40, 1888–1927. (*In* Journal of American folklore.)

Boggs, Ralph Steele. Index to Spanish folktales. . . . N. Y., Crofts, 1930. 216p.

Journal of American folklore. N. Y. Index, v. 1–40, 1888–1927.

Food

U. S. Food and drug administration. Index to notices of judgment. no. 1–date, i.e. 1–10,000, 10,001–11,000, etc. Wash., D. C., Govt. print. off.

Foreign Affairs

See **International Law and Relations; U. S. Foreign Relations.**

Foreign Trade

See **Business and Commerce.**

Forests and Forestry

Journal of forestry. Ashville, N. C., Society of American foresters. Index, v. 1–14, 1902–1916; v. 15–27, 1917–1929; v. 28–37, 1930–1939.

National shade tree conference. Proceedings. Columbus, O. Index, v. 5–10, 1929–1934; v. 11–15, 1935–1939.

Society of American foresters. Appalachian section. Proceedings. Wash., D. C. Index, v. 1–11, 1905–1916. *See also* Journal of forestry, *above*.

U. S. Forest service. Forestry, current literature, index of books and periodicals on forestry and related subjects received in Forest service library. Wash., D. C., Govt. print. off., 1934–date. (Issued by the library from May 1910 to July 1919, printed. Discontinued Sept.–Oct. 1932 to Jan. 1934.)

U. S. Forest service. Index to Fire control notes, Dec. 1936 to Oct. 1939, inclusive. Wash., D. C., Govt. print. off., 1939. 13p.

Foundry

American foundrymen's association. Transactions. Chicago. Index, v. 9–29, 1900–1921; v. 30–37, 1922–1929; v. 38–48, 1930–1940.

Fraternities

Acacia (fraternity). . . . Index to Acacia publications, 1904–1922. Ann Arbor, Mich. Subject index, member index.

Phi Delta Kappan. Fulton, Mo. Index, v. 1–20, 1915–1938.

French Language

The French review; devoted to the interests of teachers of French. N. Y. Index, v. 1–5, 1927–1932.

Friends, Society of

Friends' historical society of Philadelphia. Bulletin. Phil. Index, v. 1–10, 1906–1921; v. 11–15, 1922–1926; v. 21–25, 1932–1936.

Quaker records; being an index to "The Annual monitor," 1813–1892, containing over 20,000 obituary records, notices of members of the Society of Friends, alphabetically and chronologically arranged. Edited by Joseph J. Green. London, Hicks, 1894. 458p.

Games and Dances

*Minneapolis public library. An index to folk dances and singing games. Chicago, A.L.A., 1936. 216p.

Quigley, Marjory Closey. Index to kindergarten songs, including singing games, *see* **Children's Songs.**

Genealogy

See also **Friends, Society of; History; Wills,** Names of localities, subdivision **History.**

American genealogical index. Wesleyan University station, Middletown, Conn., 1936–1941. (Card service discontinued: v. 1 in book form to appear soon.)

Bridger, Charles. Index to printed pedigrees contained in the county and local histories, the Herald's visitations and in more important genealogical collections. London, Smith, 1867. 384p.

Daughters of the American revolution. Lineage books. Wash., D. C. Index of the rolls of honor, v. 1–40, 1890–1916; v. 41–80, 1917–1926; v. 81–120, 1928–1939.

Daughters of the American revolution magazine. A subject index of lists of revolutionary soldiers, marriage records, tombstone inscriptions, and Bible records in the D.A.R. magazine, v. 1–71, 1892–1937. Compiled by Mrs. Louise H. Rainey. N. Y., 1938.

Durrie, Daniel S. Bibliographia genealogica Americana; an alphabetical index to American genealogies and pedigrees. Albany, N. Y. Munsell, 1878. 238p.

Durrie, Daniel S. Index to genealogies. *See* Index to American genealogies, *below*.

Essex antiquarian. Salem, Mass. Index, v. 1–10, 1897–1909.

Essex institute. Historical collections, *see* **Massachusetts — History**.

Flagg, Charles A. Guide to Massachusetts local history, *see* **Massachusetts — History**.

Index to American genealogies and to genealogical material. . . . 5th ed. rev., improved and enlarged. Albany, N. Y., Munsell, 1900. 352p. Supplement, 1900–1908. 107p.

Jacobus, Donald Lines. Index to genealogical periodicals. New Haven, Conn., The author, 1932. 133p.
Supplement. p. 239–254.

Journal of American history, *see* **History**.

Koger, M. V. Index to the names of 30,000 immigrants — German, Swiss, Dutch and French into Pennsylvania, 1727–1776 by I. Daniel Rupp. pp. M. V. Koger, 1935. 232p.

Lewisiana index (to Lewisiana, or the Lewis letter). Guilford, Conn. 3v. unpaged.

McAuslan, William Alexander. Mayflower index. Boston, General society of Mayflower descendants, 1932. 2v.

Magazine of American history, *see* **History**.

Marshall, George William. The genealogist's guide. 4th ed. Guilford, Billing p.p., 1930. 880p.

Munsell's genealogical index. Albany, N .Y., Munsell, 1933. v. 1. 40p.

New England historical and genealogical register. Consolidated index, v. 1–50, 1847–1896. Boston, New England historical and genealogical society. 4v.

New York genealogical and biographical record. N. Y., Genealogical and biographical society. Index, v. 1–38, 1870–1907.

Pennsylvania German. Index to genealogical materials in the Pennsylvania German, vols. 1–13, 1900–1912. Compiled by Schuyler Lawrence. Towanda, Pa., 1937.

Sims, Richard. A manual for the genealogist, topographer and legal professor. London, Abery, 1898. 542p.

Society of colonial wars. Index of ancestors and roll of members of the Society of colonial wars. N. Y., The Society, 1922. 203p.

Stewart, Robert Armistead. Index to printed Virginia genealogies, including key and bibliography. Richmond, Va., Old dominion pr., 1930. 265p.

Stuart, Margaret. Scottish family history. A guide to works of reference on the history and genealogy of Scottish families. Edinburgh, Oliver and Boyd, 1930. 386p.

Swem, Earl G. Virginia historical index, see **Virginia — History**.

Toner, Joseph Meredith. Index to names of persons and churches in Bishop Meade's Old churches, ministers, and families of Virginia. Revised by Hugh A. Morrison. Washington, D. C., Southern history assoc., 1898. 63p.

Geography

American bureau of geography. Bulletin. Winona, Minnesota. Index, v. 1-2, with Index to Journal of geography, 1897-1921.

American geographical society of N. Y. Bulletin (formerly Journal) N. Y. Index, 1852-1915.

Association of American geographers. Annals. Albany, N. Y. Index, v. 1-25, 1911-1935, by Arthur A. Brooks.

Geographical review. N. Y. Index, v. 1-15, 1916-1925; v. 16-25, 1926-1935.

Geographical society of Philadelphia. The Bulletin. Index, v. 1-36, 1893-1939, in v. 36, p. 17-30.

Journal of geography. Syracuse, N. Y. Index, v. 1-20, 1897-1921.

Journal of school geography. Lancaster, Pa. Index, v. 1-5, 1897-1901. (*In* Index to Journal of geography.)

*National geographic magazine. Wash., D. C., National geographic society. Cumulative index, v. 1-78, 1899-1940. (Cumulative supplement issued Feb. 1st of 1942 and every year thereafter until complete new index is published.)

Skadsheim topical index to the National geographic magazine, with alphabetical and analytical sections. Chicago, Edwin Allen co., 1939, by H. Skadsheim, Berrien Springs, Michigan. unpaged.

U. S. Geographic board. Index to the fifth report, 1890-1920, and supplement, 1920-1923. Wash., D. C., Govt. print. off., 1924. 111p.

Geology

See also **Petroleum; Soils; Water**.

Albertson, George H. Geologic index of the publications of the U. S. geological survey. Denver, Col., Geological publishing co., 1931. 420p. Supplement, 1932. 15p.

American geologist. Minneapolis, Minn. Index, v. 1-36, 1888-1905.
Annotated bibliography of economic geology. Urbana, Ill. General index, v. 1-10, 1928-1938.
Economic geology. Lancaster, Pa. Index, v. 1-20, 1905-1925, by John M. Nickles; v. 21-30, 1926-1935.
Geological society of America. Bulletin. Index, v. 1-10, 1889-1900; v. 11-20, 1900-1910; v. 21-30, 1910-1919; v. 31-40, 1920-1929; v. 41-50, 1930-1939.
Journal of geology. Chicago, University of Chicago press. Index, v. 1-35, 1893-1927.
Nickles, John Milton and Robert Miller. Bibliography and index of geology exclusive of North America. Wash., D. C., Geological society of America. v. 1-1933; v. 2-4, 1933-1936; v. 5-6, 1937-1939.
U. S. Geological survey. Catalogue and index of contributions to North American geology, 1732-1891, by Nelson H. Darton. (Geological survey bulletin 127.) Wash., D. C., 1896. 1045p.
U. S. Geological survey. Catalogue and index of the publications of the Hayden, King, Powell and Wheeler surveys, by. L. F. Schmeckebier. (Geological survey bulletin 222.) Wash., D. C., Govt. print. off., 1904. 208p.
*U. S. Geological survey. Catalogue and index of the publications of the U. S. geological survey, by Philip C. Warman.
1880-1901 (Geological survey bulletin 177.) Wash., D. C., Govt. print. off., 1901, 1903. 858p.
1901-1903 (Geological survey bulletin 215.) 234p.
U. S. Geological survey. Index to Water supply papers, mineral resources of Alaska. (Water supply paper 119, 386, 430.) Wash., D. C., Govt. print. off.

Geophysics

Geophysics. Cumulative index, 1931-1939. Publications of the Society of petroleum physicists 1931-1935, Society of exploration geophysicists, 1936-1939. Houston, Texas, 1940. (Issued as v. 5, no. 3, pt. 2 of Geophysics.) 40p.
U. S. Bureau of mines. Index to geophysical abstracts, nos. 1-20, compiled by Palmer Larsen. (Information circular, no. 6589.) Wash., D. C., Govt. print. off., 1931.

Georgia — History

Georgia historical quarterly. Savannah, Ga. General index, v. 1-15, 1917-1931, compiled by Eva W. Martin.

Government Documents

See also Special subjects, i.e. **Aeronautics; Agriculture,** etc.
Ames, John Griffith. Comprehensive index to the publications of the U. S. government, 1881-1893. (58th cong., 2d sess., House doc. 754.) Wash., D. C., Govt. print. off., 1905. 2v. 1590p; 804p.

AN INDEX TO INDEXES

*Poore, Benjamin Perley. A descriptive catalogue of government publications of U. S., 1774–1881. Wash., D. C., Govt. print. off., 1885, 1392p.

U. S. Library of congress. Division of documents. Monthly checklist of state documents. Wash., D. C., Govt. print. off., 1910–date. (Annual indexes.)

U. S. National archives. Federal register. Wash., D. C., Govt. print. off. (Annual indexes.)

*U. S. Supt. of documents. Catalogue of the public documents of . . . Congress . . . (being the "Comprehensive index"). Wash., D. C., Govt. print. off., 1896–date.

*U. S. Supt. of documents. Checklist of U. S. public documents, 1789–1909, congressional: to close of 60th congress. Wash., D. C., Govt. print. off., 1911. 1707p.

U. S. Supt. of documents. Index to the reports and documents of the 54th congress, 1st sess. to 1934. Wash., D. C., Govt. print. off., 1897–1934. v. 1–43. (Being the "Consolidated index" provided for by the act of Jan. 12, 1895, with numerical lists and schedule of volumes. Discontinued July 1934.)

*U. S. Supt. of documents. Monthly catalog of U. S. public documents, 1895 to date. Wash., D. C., Govt. print. off., 1895–date. (Annual indexes.)

*U. S. Supt. of documents. Price lists. (Subject indexes.) Wash., D. C., Govt. print. off. Revised irregularly.

U. S. Supt. of documents. Tables of and annotated index to the Congressional series of U. S. public documents. Wash., D. C., Govt. print. off., 1902. 769p.

Wilcox, Jerome Kear. U. S. reference publications. Boston, Faxon, 1930. 96p.
1932 Supplement. Boston, Faxon, 1932. 135p.

Government Research

California. University. Bureau of public administration. Governmental research organization in the western states; a directory of agencies, and an index to their studies as of Jan. 1, 1939; compiled by Arthur Harris. Berkeley, Western governmental research assoc., University of California. 123p.

U. S. Federal emergency relief administration. Subject index of research bulletins and monographs issued by Federal emergency relief administration and Works progress administration, Division of social research. Wash., D. C., Govt. print. off., 1936. 119p.

U. S. Federal works agency. Index of research projects, Works progress administration, 1938–1939. Wash., D. C., Govt. print. off., 1939. 3v.

U. S. Works progress administration. Research abstracts, v. 1–2, 1939–1940. N. Y., Federal works agency, W. P. A., 1939–1940. 2 v.

Handicrafts

Becker, William J. Metal projects index. N. Y., Wilson, 1939. 34p.

Boone, Cheshire L. Guide and index to work and play books. N. Y., Doubleday, 1912. 280p.

*Lovell, Eleanor C. and Ruth M. Hall. Index to handicrafts, modelmaking and workshop projects. Boston, Faxon, 1936. 476p.

Health

See **Hygiene and Public Health.**

Highways

National research council. Highway research board. Proceedings. Wash., D. C. Index, v. 1–12, 1921–1932. Prepared by W. V. McCown and Nellie McCormick.

U. S. Bureau of public roads. Library. Highways: current literature. Wash., D. C., Govt. print. off., 1921–date. weekly.

History

See also Names of localities, subdivision **History.**

American historical association. Annual report. N. Y. Index, 1884–1914. (*In* Annual report 1914, v. 2.)

American historical association. Union list of collections in European history in American libraries, alphabetical subject index, by A. H. Shearer. Princeton, N. J., 1912–1915. 3v.

*American historical review. N. Y. General index to v. 1–10, 1895–1905 by David Maydole Matteson; v. 11–20, Oct. 1905 to July 1915; v. 21–30, Oct. 1915 to July 1925; v. 21–40, Oct. 1925 to July 1935. Prepared by Eleanor D. Smith.

American nation series. N. Y., Harper. (Analytic index, v. 28. Prepared by David Maydole Matteson.) 376p.

Annual register. General index to Dodsley's Annual register, 1758–1819. London, Baldwin, 1826. 938p.

*Cambridge modern history. N. Y., Macmillan, 1934. (General index, v. 13.)

Channing, Edward. History of the United States. N. Y., Macmillan, 1927–1930. 6v. (Supplementary volume, general index, compiled by Eva G. Moore. 1932. 155p.)

*Dictionary of American history. N. Y., Scribner, 1940. (Index, v. 6.)

Griffin, Appleton P. C. Bibliography of American historical societies, the U. S. and Canada. 2d ed. rev. and enl. Wash., D. C., 1374p. (*In* American historical association. Annual report, 1905, v. 2.) Includes index.

Griffin, Appleton P. C. Index of articles upon American local history in historical collections in the Boston public library. (*In* Boston public library bulletin, April 1883, etc.) Reprinted, 1889. 225p.

Griffin, Appleton P. C. Index of the literature of American local history in collections published in 1890–1895 (with some others). Boston, C. H. Heintzemann, 1896. 151p.

History of nations. N. Y., Collier and son, 1928. (General index, v. 25–.)
History reference council. History reference bulletin. Cambridge, Mass. Series 1, 1925–1926, and v. 1–9, 1927–1936, in v. 9, p. 141–160.
Journal of American history. New York. Index, v. 1–7, 1907–1913.
Magazine of American history. N. Y., Index, 1877–1893.
The magazine of history, with notes and queries. Tarrytown, N. Y. Index, v. 1–14, 1905–1911; v. 15–25, 1912–1917.
Extra numbers, v. 1–15, 1907–1917; v. 16–25, 1917–1924; v. 26–35, 1924–1928.
Niles' national register. Philadelphia. Index, v. 1–12, 1811–1817.
Pageant of America; a pictorial history of U. S. New Haven, Yale university press. 1925–1929. 15v. (Index in each volume.)

Holidays

*Hazeltine, Mary. Anniversaries and holidays, a calendar of days and how to observe them. Chicago, A.L.A., 1928. 308p.
Paulmier, Hazel Coddington. Index to holiday plays for schools, *see* **Children's Plays.**
Wurzburg, Dorothy A., comp. Children's short story index for special holidays, *see* **Children's Literature.**

Horticulture
See **Agriculture.**

Housing

Gries, John M. and James Ford, editors. General index to the final reports of the President's conference on home building and home ownership. Wash., D. C., President's conference on home building and home ownership, 1933. 114p.
U. S. Federal works agency. Central housing committee. Housing index-digest, June 15, 1936–date. Wash., D. C., Govt. print. off., 1936–date. Fortnightly.
U. S. Federal works agency. Central housing committee. Subcommittee on law and legislation. Housing legal digest. . . . Index of issues 1–37, Jan. 1936–Aug. 1937. Wash., D. C., 1937. 40p.

Humanities

American council of learned studies devoted to humanistic studies. Bulletin. Wash., D. C. Index to bulletins 1–10, 1920–1929.
The Harvey society. The Harvey lectures. N. Y. Index, v. 1–25, 1905–1931.
Wisconsin academy of sciences, arts and letters. Transactions. Subject and author index to the papers published by the Academy, 1870–1932, compiled by Lowell E. Noland. (*In* v. 27, p. 573–606.)

Hygiene and Public Health

See also **Medicine; Physiology; Social Hygiene,** etc.

The American journal of hygiene. Lancaster, Pa. Index to v. 1–28, 1921–1938 inclusive, compiled by Martin Frobisher, Jr.

The Journal of industrial hygiene. Baltimore. Cumulative index, v. 1–17, 1919–1936. Prepared by Helen Lawson.

Library index, a weekly index to current periodical literature in the field of public health. N. Y., National health library.

Public health nursing, see **Nursing.**

U. S. Public health service. Publications of the Public health service. Wash., D. C., Govt. print. off. (Semi-annual indexes.)

Hymns

Dearmer, Percy. Subject index to hymns in the English hymnal and songs of praise. N. Y., Oxford univ. press, 1926. 104p.

Julian, John. A dictionary of hymnology, rev. ed. with new supplement. London, Murray, 1925. 1768p. (Indexes.)

Mearns, James. Early Latin hymnaries; an index to hymns in hymnaries before 1100, with an appendix from later sources. London, Cambridge univ. press, 1913. 151p.

Richardson, Alice M. Index to stories of hymns. N. Y., Wilson, 1929. 76p.

Illinois — History

Illinois state historical library. Collections. Springfield, Ill. General index to collections, journals, publications, 1899–1928, comp. by Juliet G. Sager.

Illinois state historical society. Journal. Springfield, Ill. Index, v. 1–22, 1908–1930.

Illustrations

See **Pictures.**

Income Tax

Hartman, Dennis, ed. Income tax digest, covering v. 1–10, 11–20, 21–25 B.T.A. and decisions promulgates prior to inception of Board. Wash., D. C., Congressional press, 1931.

Hartman, Dennis, ed. Income tax index-digest of all court and treasury decisions and internal revenue rulings (prior to the inception of the Board). Wash., D. C., Legal publishing co., inc., 1930. 159p.

Hartman, Dennis, ed. Index of U. S. Board of tax appeals decisions, v. 1–20, B.T.A. (based on same index as Index-digest). Wash., D. C., Congressional press, 1928–1931. 2v.

Incunabula

Peddie, Robert Alexander. Conspectus incunabulorum; an index catalogue of the 15th century books. London, Libraco, 1910–1914. 2v.

Proctor, Robert. Index to the early printed books in the British museum from the invention of printing to the year 1500. . . . London, K. Paul, 1898–1899. 4v.

Indiana — History
Indiana magazine of history. Bloomington, Ind., Indiana univ. press. General index, v. 1–25, 1905–1929, compiled by Dorothy Riker.

Insects
See **Entomology**.

Insurance
Actuarial society of America. Transactions. N. Y. Index, v. 1–15, 1889–1914; v. 16–25, 1915–1924; v. 26–35, 1925–1934.

American institute of actuaries. The record. Chicago, Index, v. 1–15, 1909–1926; v. 16–25, 1927–1936.

Association of life insurance council. Table and index of papers presented before the association of life insurance council, 1913–1921. N. Y., Metropolitan life insurance co., 1922.

Association of life insurance presidents. Proceedings. N. Y. (A cumulative index, covering v. 1, 1907 to date has appeared every year from 1926 to 1937.)

Casualty actuarial society. Proceedings. N. Y. Index, v. 1–10, 1914–1924; v. 11–20, 1925–1934.

Factory mutual record. Boston, Mass. Index, v. 1–12, 1924–1935.

Journal of American insurance. Chicago, Ill. Index, v. 1–9, 1924–1932

Laboratories data. Chicago, Underwriters' laboratories. Index, v. 1–8, 1919–1927.

Metropolitan life insurance co. Statistical bulletin. N. Y. Cumulative index, v. 1–15, 1920–1934.

National association of insurance commissioners. Proceedings. N. Y. Index of the first 70 sessions, 1871–1939.

International Law and Relations
See also **Peace; Treaties; U. S. Foreign Relations**.

American journal of international law. N. Y. Index, v. 1–14, 1907–1920.

*Foreign affairs. N. Y. Index, v. 1–10, 1922–1932.

Hasse, Adelaide R. Index to U. S. documents relating to foreign affairs, 1828–1861. (Carnegie institution publication 185.) Wash., D. C., Carnegie institution, 1914–1921. 3v.

Inventions
See **Patents**.

Iowa — History
Annals of Iowa. Des Moines, Ia., Iowa historical dept. Index, ser. 3, v. 1–8, 1893—1909; v. 9–16, 1909–1929.

Italian Language

Italica, Bulletin of the American association of teachers of Italian. Chicago. Index, v. 1-4, 1924-1927, compiled by Vito G. Toglia.

Jews

American Jewish historical society. Publications. N. Y. Index, nos. 1-20, 1893-1914.

Central conference of American rabbis. Yearbook. Index, v. 1-50, 1890-1930.

Hasid's index to periodicals and booklist. Brooklyn, N. Y. Jan. 1932-date.

Jewish education. Chicago, National council for jewish education, Index, v. 1-6, Jan. 1929 - Dec. 1934.

Jewish frontier. N. Y. Index, v. 2-6, Dec. 1934-Dec. 1939.

Jewish quarterly review. Philadelphia. Classified index to v. 1-20, 1909-1930. new series.

Kansas — Politics and Government

Kansas government journal. Lawrence, Kansas, League of Kansas municipalities. Index, v. 1-8, 1914-1922.

Kentucky — History

Kentucky state historical society. Register. Frankfort, Ky. Index, v. 1-20, 1903-1922.

Labor

American federationalist. N. Y. Index, v. 1-21, 1894-1914.

American labor legislation review. N. Y. American association for labor legislation. Index, v. 1-20, 1911-1930.

Illinois state federation of labor. Weekly news letter. Chicago. Index, v. 1-14, 1915-Mr. 30, 1929.

Law and labor. N. Y., League for industrial rights. Decennial index. v. 1-10, 1919-1928.

Rand school of social science. Labor research dept. Index to labor articles, N. Y., Rand, 1926-date. monthly.

U. S. Bureau of labor statistics. Cumulative index to U. S. Bureau of labor statistics bulletins on court decisions, 1912-1932, with brief of cases. *In* Bulletin 592:321-387. 1933.

U. S. Bureau of labor statistics. Monthly labor review: subject index, v. 1-11, July 1915-Dec. 1920, prepared by Karoline Klager and Elsie M. Pursglove. Wash., D. C., Govt. print. off., 1923. 176p.

U. S. Bureau of labor statistics. Subject index of the publications of the Bureau of labor statistics up to May 1, 1915. (Bulletin 174: Miscellaneous series, 11.) Wash., D. C., Govt. print. off., 1915. 233p.

U. S. Dept. of labor. Index of all reports issued by bureaus of labor statistics in the U. S. prior to March 1, 1902. Wash., D. C., Govt. print. 1902. 287p.

Lands

See also **Soils.**

U. S. General land office. Index to Circulars and publications of the General land office. Wash., D. C., Govt. print. off., 1928. 48p.

U. S. General land office. Index to Circulars and regulations of the General land office issued since Jan. 1930. Wash., D. C., Govt print. off., 1932. 13p.

Landscape Gardening

Landscape architecture. Cambridge, Mass., American society of landscape architects. Index, v. 1–20, 1910–1930.

Language and Languages

See also **French Language; Italian Language; Spanish Language; Speech.**

American journal of philology. Baltimore. Index, v. 1–10, 1880–1889 in v. 19, p. 515–538; v. 11–20, 1890–1899 in v. 20, p. 471–483; v. 21–30, 1900–1909 in v. 30, p. 487–504; v. 31–40, 1910–1919 in v. 40, p. 546–472; v. 41–60, 1920–1939 in v. 60, p. 519–560.

Classical philology. Chicago, Univ. of Chicago. General index, by authors and subjects, v. 1–10, 1906–1915, compiled by F. E. Robbins.

Language. Baltimore, Linguistic society of America. Index, v. 1–5, 1925–1929; v. 6–10, 1930–1934; v. 11–15, 1935–1939.

Modern language association of America. Publications. Menasha, Wisc. Index, v. 1–50, 1884–1935; v. 51–55, 1936–1940.

Modern language notes. Baltimore. General index, v. 1–50, 1886–1935.

Latin America

See also **Pan American Union.**

Grismer, Raymond L. A reference index to 12,000 Spanish-American authors, *see* **Authors.**

Inter-American book exchange. Index to Latin-American books, v. 1, 1938, edited by Raul d'Eca. Wash., D. C., Inter-American book exchange, 1940. 484p.

Law

See also Special subjects, i.e. **Business Law; Crime and Criminals.**

— **Constitutions and Statutes**

Columbia university. Legislative drafting research fund. Index digest of state constitutions. Albany, N. Y., N. Y. state library, Univ. of the state of N. Y., 1915. 1546p.

The Constitution of the United States of America (annotated). Annotations of cases decided by the Supreme court of the U. S. to Jan. 1, 1938. (Senate document no. 232.) Wash., D. C., Govt. print. off., 1938. 1246p. (Index, p. 1181–1246.)

New York (state). Constitutional convention committee. (Mott and Hindman) Constitutions of the states and United States. Albany, N. Y., J. B. Lyon, 1938. 1845p. (Index, p. 1741–1813.)

New York state library. Index of legislation, 1890–1908. Albany, N. Y. (Beginning with 1903, the Index and other legislative bulletins of each year are reissued in 1 volume under title: Yearbook of legislation. Title varies: 1890–1894, Comparative summary and index of state legislation by states; 1901–1904, Comparative summary and index of legislation; 1905, Index of legislation.)

Public affairs information service, see **Public Affairs**.

U. S. Laws, statutes. Index to the federal statutes (1789–1873, 1874–1931) general and permanent law . . . Wash., D. C., Govt. print. off., 1911–1933. 1432p. (1789–1873 indexes v. 1–17 of the Statutes at large; 1874–1931 indexes the Revised statutes of 1874 and the Statutes at large, v. 18–46; latter volume is revision of Scott and Beaman's Index analysis. Includes an index of popular names.)

U. S. Library of congress. Legislative reference service. State law index and digest to the legislation of the states of the U. S. enacted . . . Wash., D. C., Govt. print. off., 1925/26–to date. (8th biennial volume, 1939–1940.)

Note: Many states have separate indexes to their bills and statutes, which are more detailed and cover longer periods than the above.

— Digests and Reports

American digest. Descriptive-word index to the 1st and 2d decennial digests. St. Paul, West pub. co., 1924. 3070p. Descriptive-word index, covering 3d and 4th decennial digests. St. Paul, West publishing co., 1940. 2v.

Descriptive-word index, covering v. 1–10. St. Paul, West publishing co., 1940. 1230p. (4th decennial volume includes a table of popular names of cases.)

American law reports annotated. Complete word-index of annotations in American law reports, covering v. 1–100. A.L.R. with pocket supplement continuations. San Francisco, Calif., Bancroft-Whitney co., 1931. 3v.

Note: There are also many other digest indexes, but so seldom helpful that they are unnecessary in this list.

— Table of Cases

American digest tables of cases. St. Paul, West pub. co., 1911– . (The "Tables of cases" for the various units of the American digest list all state and federal cases decided by the higher courts.)

— Encyclopedias

Corpus juris. Descriptive word-index. N. Y., American law book co., 1937. 3639p.

Ruling case law. Complete R.C.L. index; master index of the matter in R.C.L. v. 1–28, R.C.L. permanent supplements, 8v, and R.C.L. supplement 1930 and later, by Joseph H. Hill and publishers' editorial staff. . . . Northport, N. Y., Edward Thompson co., 1931. 2v.

— Periodicals

American association of law libraries. Index to legal periodicals, 1908–date. (Published in conjunction with the Law library journal.) N. Y., Wilson, 1909–date. (Annual to 1925, since then triennial cumulative quarterly advance numbers.)

Current legal thought; selected and abstracted from the law reviews of the day. N. Y. Annual cumulative indexes; monthly current indexes. v. 1, 1935–date.

Jones, Leonard A. and Chipman, George E. Index to legal periodicals. Boston, Chipman. 6v. (covers earliest periodical literature to 1937). (Special volume for 1923–1927 connects with Commerce clearing house legal periodicals digest for 1928–date.)

Legal periodical digest of current articles involving research in all law periodicals published in the English language. N. Y., Commerce clearing house, inc., 1928–date.

Note: In addition to above general periodical indexes, many law magazines have separate detailed indexes. The following seem to merit special mention:

American bar association. Journal. Baltimore. Topical index, v. 1–23, 1915–1937.

California law review. Berkeley. Cumulative index, v. 1–25, 1912–1922.

Central law journal. St. Louis, Mo. Index-digest, v. 1–54, 1874–1902.

Columbia law review. N. Y. Cumulative index, v. 1–30, 1900–1930; supplement, v. 31–35, 1931–1935.

Green bag. Boston. General index, v. 1–26, 1889–1914.

Harvard law review. Cambridge, Mass. Cumulative index, v. 1–30, 1887–1937.

Illinois law review. Chicago. Cumulative index, v. 1–10, 1906–1916; v. 11–25, 1916–1931.

Michigan law review. Ann Arbor. Index, v. 1–20, 1902–1922. (Current issues include monthly index to all legal literature.)

Yale law journal. New Haven. Index, v. 1–38, 1891–1929; v. 39–43, 1929–1934.

— Maxims

Broom, Herbert. A selection of legal maxims. 10th ed. by R. H. Kersley. London, Swett and Maxwell, 1939. 706p.

Corpus juris secundum. Brooklyn, America law book co., 1936–date. (v. 27, 1941.)

League of Nations

Carroll, Marie J. Key to League of nations documents placed on public sale, 1920–1929. Boston, World peace foundation, 1930. 340p. Supplements 1930, 1931, 1932–1933.

League of nations. Index bibliographicus: international catalogue of sources of current bibliographical information. Boston, World peace foundation, 1925. 233p.

League of nations. Economic committee. Index to the reports, first session, Nov. 1920 to the thirtieth session, Nov. 1929, and of the Economic consultative committee (1st session, May 1928 and 2d session, May 1929). Boston, World peace foundation, 1931. 33p.

League of nations. Financial committee. Index (Report to the council on work of the 24-27 sessions of the committee) together with relevant resolutions of council; first session, Nov. 1920, to 25th session, Dec. 1926. Boston, World peace foundation, 1928. 32p.

League of nations. International committee on intellectual cooperation. Index to the minutes of the committee sessions, v. 5-7, 7-11, 1926-1930. Boston, World peace foundation, 1927-1931.

League of nations. Permanent mandate commission. General index to the records of the commission, no. 3 (session 11-20, 1927-1931). Boston, World peace foundation, 1931. 67p.

League of nations. Treaty series. General indexes, no. 1-6, v. 1-152, 1927-1933. Paris, Berger and Levault.

Wendelin, Eric C. Subject index to the economic and financial documents of the League of nations, 1927-1930. Boston, World peace foundation, 1932. 190p.

Leather

American leather chemists association. Journal, *see* **Chemistry.**

Library Science

See also **Bibliography.**

Burton, Margaret and Marion E. Vosburgh. Bibliography of librarianship, classified and annotated guide to the library literature of the world.... London, Library association, 1934. 176p.

Cannons, Harry George T. Bibliography of library economy, 1876-1920. Chicago, A.L.A., 1927. 680p. (Followed by Library literature.)

The Catholic library world. Chestnut Hill, Mass., Boston college library. Index to v. 1-6, Dec. 1929 to June 1935.

Current library literature, 1929-1930; a subject index to library material recorded in those two years, reprinted from Library journal. N. Y., Bowker, 1931. 41p.

Library journal. N. Y. General index, v. 1-22, 1876-1897.

Library literature, 1921-1932 . . . compiled by the Junior members round table of the A.L.A., under the editorship of Lucile Morsch. Chicago, A.L.A., 1934. 430p.

Library literature, 1933/1935-date . . . an author and subject index-digest. N. Y., Wilson, 1936. 435p.

Library literature, 1936-1939. N. Y., Wilson, 1940. 1748p.

Library magazine. N. Y. Index, 1879-1887, v. 1-v. 2, ser. 3.

AN INDEX TO INDEXES

The library quarterly. Chicago, University of Chicago press. Index, v.1–5, 1931–1935, compiled by Mary L. McEldowney; v. 6–10, 1936–1940, compiled by Mildred G. Bosworth.

Library work cumulated, 1905–1911. N. Y., Wilson, 1912. 409p.

Moody, Katharine Twining. Index to library reports. Chicago, A.L.A., 1913. 185p.

New York libraries. Albany, N. Y. Index, v. 1–10, 1907–1927.

New York public library. Bulletin. N. Y. Index to v. 1–40, 1897–1936, compiled and edited by Daniel C. Haskell.

Special libraries association. Special libraries. N. Y. Cumulative index, v. 1–13, 1910–1922; v. 14–17, 1923–1926.

Towner, Isabel L., comp. Cumulative index to v. 1–10 of Classics of American librarianship. N. Y., Wilson, 1933. 151p.

Wilson library bulletin; a magazine for librarians. N. Y., Wilson co. Index, v. 1–5, 1914–1931 (June).

Lincoln, Abraham

Abraham Lincoln association. Annual papers. Springfield, Ill. Index, 1924–1928 (issued as Lincoln centennial assoc. papers); 1929–1939 (issued as Abraham Lincoln association papers).

Literature

See also **Drama**; **Essays**; **Poetry**, etc.

A.L.A. index; an index to general literature. 2d ed. enl. and brought down to Jan. 1, 1900. Boston, A.L.A. publishing board, 1901. 679p. Supplement, 1900–1910. Chicago, A.L.A., 1914. 223p.

American prefaces. Iowa city, Ia. Elmhurst, Ill., Elmhurst college library. Index, v. 1–5, 1935–1940.

Annals of English literature, 1475–1925; the principal publications of each year with an alphabetical index of authors and their works. Oxford, Clarendon press, 1935. 340p. (Detailed author index, p. 268–340.)

Annual library index, 1905–1910. N. Y., Publishers' weekly, 1906–1911. 6v.

Annual literary index, 1892–1904. N. Y., Publishers' weekly, 1893–1905. 13v.

Bibelot. Portland, Oregon. Index, v. 1–20, 1890–1914.

Burr, Allston. Sir Walter Scott; an index placing the short poems in his novels and in his long poems and dramas. Cambridge, Harvard, 1936. 130p.

*Cambridge history of American literature. N. Y., Putnam, 1921. (Index, v. 4, p.829–872.)

*Cambridge history of English literature. N. Y., Macmillan, 1933. 413p. (General index, v. 15.)

Cook, Edward T. and Alexander Wedderburn. General index to the works of John Ruskin. (Works of Ruskin, ed. by E. T. Cook and A. Wedderburn, v. 39.) London, Allen, 1912. 689p.

Gillette, Fredericka B. Title index to the works of Honoré de Balzac. (Bulletin of bibliography pamphlets, 19.) Boston, Boston book co., 1909. 24p.

Harvard classics edited by Charles W. Eliot, N. Y., P. F. Collins and son, 1909–1910. 50v. (Index in v. 50.)

Index to "Little classics" series. Huntington Free library, 9 Westchester square, N. Y. city.

Manly, John Matthews and Edith Rickert. Contemporary American literature bibliographies and study outlines; introduction and revision by Fred B. Millett. N. Y., Harcourt, 1929. 378p.

Manly, John Matthews and Edith Rickert. Contemporary British literature bibliographies and study outlines. N. Y., Harcourt, 1928. 345p.

O'Connor, Evangeline M. Analytical index to the works of Nathaniel Hawthorne. Boston, Houghton, 1882. 294p.

Patterson, Frank Allen. An index to the Columbia edition of the works of John Milton, by Frank Allen Patterson, assisted by French Rowe Fogle. N. Y., Columbia univ. press, 1940. 2v.

Saxton, Eugene F. The Kipling index. N. Y., Doubleday, 1911. 44p.

Sears, Minnie Earl and Marian Shaw. Essay and general literature index, *see* **Essays.**

Southern literary messenger. Charlottesville, Va. Index, v. 1–38, 1834–1864.

Walbridge, Earle. Index and key to "Literary characters drawn from life." N. Y., Wilson, 1938. 32p.

Warner library. N. Y., Warner library co., 1917. (General index, v. 30.)

Wells, Goeffrey H. The works of H. G. Wells, 1887–1925. A bibliography, dictionary and subject-index. N. Y., Wilson, 1926. 274p.

White, Beatrice. An index to the Elizabethan stage and William Shakespeare; a study of facts and problems by Sir Edmund Chambers. Oxford, Clarendon press, 1934. 161p.

Yale literary magazine. New Haven, Conn. Index, v. 1–32, 1832–1868.

Machinery

American machinist. N. Y. Index, v. 7–27, 1884–1904.

Machinery's encyclopedia. N. Y., Industrial pr., 1917. (v. 7 includes Index.)

Massachusetts — History

Colonial society of Mass. Publications. Boston. Index, v. 1–25, 1892–1924.

Danvers historical society. Historical collections. Danvers, Mass. Index to v. 1–5, 1913–1917; v. 6–20, 1918–1932.

Essex antiquarian, *see* **Genealogy.**

Essex institute. Historical collections. Salem, Mass. Index, v. 1–57, 1859–1931.

Flagg, Charles A. Guide to Massachusetts local history, being a bibliographic index. . . . Salem, Mass., Salem press co., 1907. 256p.

Massachusetts. Historical society. Proceedings. Boston, Mass. Index to second series, v. 1-20, 1884-1907.

Mathematics

See also **Accounting; Statistics.**

American journal of mathematics. Baltimore. Index, v. 1-50, 1878-1928.

American mathematical society. Bulletin. Lancaster, Pa. General index, s2, v. 1-10, 1891-1904; v. 11-20, 1904-1914; v. 21-30, 1914-1924; v. 31-40, 1925-1934.

American mathematical society. Transactions, Lancaster, Pa. Index, v. 1-20, 1900-1919; v. 21-30, 1920-1928.

Annals of mathematics. Princeton, N. J. Index, v. 1-12, 1884-1899; v. 1-12, 1900-1911 (series 2).

Mathematics teacher. N. Y., National council of teachers. Index, v. 14-21, 1921-1929.

Mechanical Engineering

American society of mechanical engineers. Transactions. N. Y. Index, v. 1-45, 1880-1923.

Medicine

See also **Anatomy; Bacteriology; Dentistry; Hygiene and Public Health; Nursing; Pharmacology; Physiology; Psychology.**

American journal of orthopsychiatry. Menasha, Wisconsin. Index, v. 1-10, 1930-1940, compiled by Victoria Sloane.

American medical association. Journal. Chicago. Index, v. 1-24, 1883-1906.

American observer medical monthly Detroit, Mich. Index, v. 1-10, 1864-1873.

American review of tuberculosis. N. Y., National tuberculosis assoc. Cumulative index, v. 1-34, March 1917-Dec. 1936.

American surgical association. Transactions. Philadelphia. Index, v. 1-26, 1880-1906.

Archives of otology. N. Y. Each 7th volume includes index. (v. 1-1869.)

Association of American medical colleges. Proceedings. Index, no. 1-33, 1891-1923.

Association of American physicians. Transactions. Philadelphia. Index, v. 1-30, 1886-1915.

Chapin, William D., comp. Index to original communications in the medical journals of the United States and Canada for 1877-1878. Classified by subjects and authors. N. Y., 1878-1879. 2v.

Clinical abstracts; medical and surgical articles of outstanding value with index cumulated weekly, abstracted from leading American and foreign periodicals, v. 1–2, 1939–1941. N. Y., and London, Keesing, 1939–1941. In progress.

French, Herbert, ed. Index of differential diagnosis of main symptoms (medical and surgical) 5th ed. Baltimore, Wood, 1936. 1145p.

Hutchesin, Sir Robert and Reginald Hilton. Index of treatment; articles by 78 leading authorities. 12th ed. Baltimore, Wood, 1940. 1012p.

Index-abstract of surgical technique. N. Y. v. 1–17, 1903–1917. (v. 1 no. 1 as Index abstract of sterile surgery.)

Index medicus; a quarterly classified record of the current medical literature of the world, 1879–1927. Wash., D. C., Carnegie institute, 1879–1927. 45p.
v. 1–21, Jan. 1879–April 1899; 1st ser.
v. 1–18, Jan. 1903–Dec. 1920; 2d ser.
v. 1–6, Jan. 1921–June 1927; 3d ser.
(United with Quarterly cumulative index to current medical lit. to form Quarterly cumulative index medicus.)

Index medicus . . . War supplement, a classified record of literature on military medicine and surgery, 1914–1917. Wash., D. C., Carnegie institute, 1917.

Journal of experimental medicine. N. Y., Rockefeller inst. for medical research, 1916. Index, v. 1–20, 1896–1914; v. 21–40, 1915–1924.

Journal of infectious diseases. Chicago, Memorial institute for infectious diseases. Index, v. 1–15, 1904–1914.

Journal of medical research. Boston. Index, v. 1–30, 1896–1914; v. 31–44, 1914–1924.

Journal of nervous and mental diseases. N. Y. General index of subjects, v. 1–50, 1874–1919, prepared by Smith Ely Jelliffe.

Journal of urology. Baltimore, American urological assoc. Index, v. 1–10, 1917–1923; v. 11–20, 1924–1928.

Leftwich, Ralph W. An index of symptoms with diagnostic methods. 5th ed. N. Y., Wood, 1915. 555p.

Medical annual, general index, 1925–1934. Bristol, J. Wright, 1934.

Opthalmic record. Nashville, Tenn. Index, v. 1–21, 1891–1912.

Oto-laryngology. Chicago. Index, v. 1–7, 1911–1917.

Oxford medicine. Index. N. Y., Oxford univ. press, 1928. 267p. (Index, v. 8.)

Pan-therapist. Chicago. Index, v. 1–18, 1851–1870.

Quarterly cumulative index medicus. Chicago, American medical association, 1927–date.

Rockefeller institute for medical research. Studies. N. Y. Index, v. 1–25, 1904–1916; v. 25–50, 1917–1924; v. 51–116, 1924–1940.

Short, Arthur R., ed. An index of prognosis and end-results of treatment, by various authors. 3d ed. rev. and enl. N. Y., Wood, 1915.

AN INDEX TO INDEXES

Society of medical history of Chicago. Bulletin. Chicago. Index, v. 1–4, 1911–1935.

Surgery, gynecology and obstetrics. Chicago. Index, v. 1–40, 1905–1925 including index to International abstract of surgery beginning with 1915.

Tidy, Henry L. Index of symptomatology, by various authors. Bristol, Wright, 1928. 722p.

U. S. Naval medical bulletin. Wash., D. C., U. S. Bureau of medicine and surgery. Index, v. 1–26, 1907–1928.

U. S. Surgeon-general's office. Index catalogue of the library. Wash., D. C., Govt. print. off.
1st series, 1880–1895. 16v.
2d series, 1896–1915. 21v.
3d series, 1918–1932. 10v.
4th series, 1936–date.

Metals
See **Mining and Metallurgy.**

Michigan — History
Michigan. Historical commission. Historical collections. Lansing. Index, v. 1–39, 1874–1915.

Microscopy
American microscopical society. Transactions. Lancaster, Pa. Index, v. 1–25, 1878–1903.

American monthly microscopical journal. N. Y. Index, v. 1–15, 1880–1894; v. 16–17, 1895–1896.

Microscopical bulletin and science news. Philadelphia. Index, v. 1–6, 1883–1889.

Military Science
See also **Naval Science; Selective Service.**

Field artillery journal. Wash., D. C., U. S. Field artillery assoc. Index, v. 1–6, 1911–1915.

International military digest; a review of the current literature of military science for 1915–1918. Cumulated from the monthly issues of the International military digest. N. Y., Cumulative digest corporation, 1916–1919. 4v.

U. S. War dept. Index of U. S. army and federal specifications used by the War dept., Jan. 1941. 261p.

U. S. War dept. Index to General orders, Bulletins and numbered Circulars, War dept., 1920–39. Wash., D. C., Govt. print. off., 1940. 38p.

U. S. War dept. Adjutant general's office. Analytical index to General orders, Adjutant general's office, 1861–1876. Wash., D. C., Govt. print. off., 1878.

U. S. War dept. Adjutant general's office. Index to army regulations and changes promulgated prior to Oct. 1, 1930. Prepared under the direction of the Adjutant general. (Army regulation no. 1–5.) Wash., D. C., Govt. print. off., 1930.

U. S. War dept. Adjutant general's office. Subject index of General orders of the War dept., Jan. 1, 1809–Dec. 31, 1860. Jan. 1, 1881–Dec. 31, 1900. Wash., D. C., Govt. print. off., 1886, 1901.

U. S. War dept. Office of Judge advocate general. Consolidated index of unpublished volumes of opinions and of digests of opinions of the Judge advocate general of the Army, 1912–1924. Wash., D. C., Govt. print. off., 1926. 352p.

U. S. War dept. Office of the chief of air corps. Index to unrestricted Army air corps information circulars. Wash., D. C., 1928. (Inf. circular v. 6, no. 600, May 15, 1928.)
Supplement, nos. 601–657 inclusive. Jan. 15, 1931.

U. S. War dept. Ordnance bureau. Index to Ordnance pamphlets with notes relating to their use and distribution, Nov. 1905–June 1923. (Ordnance pamphlet O.) Wash., D. C., Govt. print. off., 54p.

U. S. War dept. Ordnance bureau. Index to reports of the Chief of ordnance, Army, 1864–1912. Wash., D.C., Govt. print. off., 1913. 193p.

Mining and Metallurgy
See also **Geophysics.**

American institute of mining and metallurgical engineers. Transactions. N. Y. Index, v. 1–35, 1871–1904; v. 36–40, 1905–1916; v. 56–72, 1917–1925; v. 73–117, 1926–1935.

The American mineralogist. Menasha, Wisconsin. Index to v. 1–20, 1916–1935, by John Milton Nickles.

American society for metals. Transactions. Cleveland, O. Index, v. 1–10, 1920–1926.

Appalachian coals, incorp. Proceedings. Index, 1st conference, Sept. 12, 1934 to 22d conference, Feb. 8, 1938. In 4 pts.

Crane, Walter Richard. Index of mining engineering literature, comprising an index of mining, metallurgical, civil, mechanical, electrical, and chemical engineering subjects as related to mining engineering. N. Y., Wiley, 1909–1912. 2v.

Granite monthly. Concord, N. H. Index, v. 1–34, 1877–1903.

Kinsev, V. E. and T. E. Hopkins. Index to iron and steel patents, see **Patents.**

Metal progress. Cleveland, O., American society for steel treating. Index, v. 1–10, 1920–1926.

Metals and alloys. N. Y. Cumulative index of Metallurgical abstracts, published in v. 1 and 2 of Metals and alloys, July 1929–Dec. 1931.

AN INDEX TO INDEXES 45

Mining and metallurgical society of America. Bulletin. N. Y. 25th anniversary index, v. 1–26, 1908–1933. (Complete index to all volumes. ... Transactions and Bulletins issued by the society since its founding.)

Mining world index of current literature. Chicago, Mining world co. v. 1–10, 1912–1916.

Smithsonian institution. Index to the literature of gallium, 1874–1903, by Phillip E. Browning. (Misc. coll. v. 66, no. 1543.) Wash., D. C., Govt. print. off., 1904. 12p.

Smithsonian institution. Index to the literature of germanium, 1886–1903, by Philip E. Browning. (Misc. coll. v. 66, no. 1544.) Wash., D. C., Govt. print. off., 1904. 8p.

Smithsonian institution. Index to the literature of indium, 1863–1903. by Philip E. Browning. (Misc. coll. v. 66, no. 1571.) Wash., D. C., Govt. print. off., 1905. 15p.

U. S. Bureau of mines. Index of papers published in the technical press, July 1, 1910 to Dec. 31, 1930, compiled by H. C. Carroll, Wash., D. C., Govt. print. off., 1931. 2v.

U. S. Bureau of mines. Index of publications, July 1925. Subject index of Bureau of mines reports of investigations published 1919–1924. Wash., D. C., Govt. print. off., 1925. 35p.

U. S. Bureau of mines. List of publications, Bureau of mines, complete from establishment, 1910 to June 30, 1937 with subject index. Wash., D. C., Govt. print. off., 1939. 356p. Supplement, 1939–1940.

Minnesota — History

Minnesota historical society. St. Paul, Minn. Collections. Index, v. 1–10, 1850–1905.

Mississippi River and Valley

Mississippi river commission. Index of reports, 1879–1895. Wash., D. C., Govt. print. off., 1896. 100p.

Mississippi valley historical review. Cedar Rapids, Iowa. Topical guide to v. 1–19, 1914–1932, and to Proceedings, v. 1–11, 1907–1924. Cumulative index to v. 16–25, June 1929 through March 1939, compiled by Bertha E. Josephson.

Missouri — History

Missouri historical review. Columbia, Mo., Index, v. 1–25, Oct. 1906–July 1931, compiled by the Columbia library club.

Monologs

*Ireland, Norma Olin and David E. Ireland. Index to monologs and dialogs. Boston, Faxon, 1939. 127p.

46 AN INDEX TO INDEXES

Motion Pictures

Cook, Dorothy E. and E. C. Rahbek-Smith. Educational film catalog, a classified list of 1175 non-theatrical films with separate title and subject index. N. Y., Wilson, 1939. 332p.

1940 supplement. N. Y., Wilson, 1940. 111p.

Film index, a bibliography; v. 1, the film as art; compiled by the workers of the Writers' program of the W. P. A. in the city of N. Y. N. Y., Museum of modern art film library and Wilson co., 1941. 723p.

Motion picture review digest. N. Y., Wilson. 1936–1940.

Society of motion picture engineers. Journal. Easton, Pa. Index, v. 1–14, no. 6, 1916–1930.

Mountaineering

Appalachia. Boston. Index, v. 1–10, 1876–1904.

Trail and timberline. Denver, Colorado mountain club. Index, no. 1–146. 1918–1930.

Municipal Engineering

American society of municipal engineers and International association of public works officials. Proceedings. Chicago. Index, 1918–1936.

Municipal Government

Mind your business; bulletin of the Bureau of municipal research. St. Louis, Municipal reference library. Index, no. 1–91, 1923–1932.

Municipal index, 1924–date. N. Y., American city, 1924–date.

Western city. Los Angeles, Calif. Index, v. 9–13, 1923–1937, prepared by the Bureau of municipal research and service, University of Oregon.

Museums

See also **National Museum; Natural History.**

American association of museums. Index to publications of the American association of museums. Completed serials: proceedings of the A.A.M., 1907–1917; Museum work, 1918–1926. (Publications of the A.A.M., n.s., no. 2.) Wash., D. C., 1927. 34p.

Boston. Museum of fine arts. Bulletin. Index, v. 1–13, 1903–1915; v. 14–23, 1916–1925.

Milwaukee. Public museum. Yearbook. Milwaukee, Wisconsin. Index, v. 1–10, 1921–1930.

New York. Metropolitan museum of art. Annual reports. N. Y. Index, 1871–1902, 1902–1912, 1912–1921, 1922–1931.

New York. Metropolitan museum of art. Bulletin. N. Y. Index, v. 1–22, 1905–1927.

New York state museum. Annual reports. N. Y. Index, v. 1–20, 1847–1902.

St. Louis. City art museum. Bulletin. St. Louis, Mo. Index, v. 1–14, 1914–1929.

Worcester art museum. Bulletin. Worcester, Mass. Index, v. 1–6, 1910–1916.

Music

See also **Ballads; Children's Songs; Hymns; Operas; Songs.**

Blom, Eric. General index to modern musical literature in the English language including periodicals for the years 1915–1926. Philadelphia, Curwen, 1927. 159p.

Modern music. N. Y. Index, v. 1–12, 1924–1935.

Musical quarterly. N. Y. Index of authors and subjects for v. 1–10, 1915–1924.

Mythology

*Frazer, James G. The golden bough. London, Macmillan. (Index, v. 12, p. 147–536.)

*Mythology of all races. N. Y., Archaeological institute of America. (Index, v. 13.) 477p.

National Museum

U. S. National museum. List of publications, with index to titles. Wash., D. C., Govt. print. off., 1902–1914.
1875–1900 (Bulletin 151) 168p.
1901–1906 (Bulletin 51, supp.) 40p.
1906–1912. 41p.

National Resources

U. S. National planning board, National resources board, National resources committee. Subject index of reports. Wash., D. C., Natl. resources planning board, 1940. 76p.

Natural History

See also **Botany; Horticulture; Ornithology.**

Altsheler, Brent. Natural history index-guide. 3d ed., rev. and enl. N. Y., Wilson, 1940. 583p.

American museum of natural history. Bulletin. N. Y. Index, v. 1–16, 1881–1902.

American museum of natural history. Memoirs. N. Y., v. 1–7, 1893–1902.

Cincinnati society of natural history. Journal. Cincinnati, O. Index, v. 1–10, 1878–1888, including index to Proceedings.

Ellis, Jessie Croft. Nature index, *see* **Pictures.**

Ellis, Mary. Index to publications of N. Y. state natural history survey and N. Y. state museum, 1837–1902. Albany, N. Y., State education dept., 1903.

Nature magazine. Wash., D. C., American nature association. Ten-year index, v. 1–20, 1923–1932, compiled and edited by Edward A. Preble.

New England museum of natural history. Bulletin. Boston. Index, no. 1–50, 1915–1928.

Naval Science

American society of naval engineers. Journal. Wash., D. C. Index, v. 1–16, 1889–1904.

Society of naval architects and marine engineers. Transactions. N. Y. Index, v. 1–38, 1893–1930.

U. S. Dept. of commerce. American marine standards commission. American marine standard lists and indexes. Wash., D. C., Govt. print. off., 1931. 9p.

U. S. Hydrographic office. General catalog of mariners' charts and books, to Jan. 1941. Wash., D. C., Govt. print. off., 1941. 169p. and tables.

U. S. Naval institute. Proceedings. Annapolis, Md. Classified analytical index, March 1902–Oct. 1919.

U. S. Navy dept. Cumulative index to Court-martial orders for the years 1916–1937. Wash., D. C., Govt. print. off., 1940. 840p.

Negroes

Norfolk journal and guide, *see* **Newspapers**.

New England

See also names of New England states, i.e. **Massachusetts**.

New England historical and genealogical register, *see* **Genealogy**.

The New England quarterly. Boston. General index to v. 1–10, 1928–1937.

New Englander, *see* **Periodicals, General**.

Society for the preservation of New England antiquities. Old-time New England, *see* **Antiquities**.

New Jersey — History

New Jersey historical society. Documents relating to the colonial history of the state of New Jersey. Index, v. 1–10, 1880–1886.

New Jersey historical society. Proceedings. Index, 1845–1919.

New York — History

Dutchess co. historical society. Yearbook. Poughkeepsie, N. Y. Index, 1914–1927, 1928–1931, 1934–1939.

New York genealogical and biographical record, *see* **Genealogy**.

New York state historical association. New York history. Index, v. 1–6, 1919–1925, v. 7–16, 1926–1935.

AN INDEX TO INDEXES 49

New York state historical association. Proceedings. Albany, N. Y. Index, v. 1-23, 1901-1925.

Rochester historical society. Publication fund series. Rochester, N. Y. General index, v. 1-14, 1922-1937.

Newspapers

New York daily tribune index, 1875-1906. 31v.

*New York times index, 1851-1860, 1863-1905, 1913-date. N. Y., 1913-date.

Norfolk journal and guide. News index, 1936-date. Norfolk, Va. The guide publishing co., 1936-date.

Times, London. Palmer's index to the Times newspaper, 1790-date. London, Palmer, 1868-date.

Times, London. Quarterly index to the London Times, 1906-date. London, Times office, 1906-date (Official index).

U. S. Daily. Index to the U. S. Daily, v. 1-6, 1926/27-1931/32. Wash., D. C., Daily pub. corp.

North Carolina — History

North Carolina booklet — Great events in North Carolina History. Raleigh, N. C. Index, v. 1-20, 1901-1921.

Northwest

Judson, Katherine Berry. Subject index to the history of the Pacific Northwest and of Alaska... Olympia, Wash., Lamborn, 1913. 341p.

Pacific northwest quarterly. Seattle, Wash. Guide to the Washington historical quarterly and the Pacific Northwest quarterly, 1906-1938, v. 1-29, by Jessie S. Douglas. *In* v. 29, p. 337-416.

U. S. Geological survey. Index to Water supply papers, mineral resources of Alaska, *see* Geology.

Numismatics

American journal of numismatics. N. Y., American numismatic society. Index, v. 1-50, 1866-1916.

Nursing

American journal of nursing. N. Y. Cumulative index, v. 1-10, Oct. 1900-Sept. 1910; v. 11-20, Oct. 1910-Sept. 1920; v. 21-30, Oct. 1920-Dec. 1930.

Public health nursing. N. Y., Natl. assoc. for public health nursing. N. Y. Index, v. 1-6, 1909-1914.

Nutrition

See also Food.

Journal of nutrition. Springfield, Ill. General index, v. 1-15, 1928-1939.

Occupations
See **Vocations**.

Ohio — History
Firelands pioneer. Norwalk, O., Firelands historical society. Index, v. 1. no. 1 old ser.–v. 20 new ser., June 1858–1937.

Ohio state archaeological and historical society. Ohio archaeological and historical quarterly. Columbus, O. Index, v. 1–43, 1887–1934.

Overman, William D. Index to materials for study of Ohio history. (*In* Ohio state archaeological and historical quarterly, v. 44, p. 138–155. 1935.)

Operas
Rieck, Waldemar. Opera plots. An index to the stories of operas, operettas, etc. from the 16th to the 20th century. N. Y., New York public library, 1927. 102p.

Optics
Optical society of America. Journal. N. Y., American institute of physics, 1936. Index, v. 1–25, 1917–1935.

Orations
Brewer, David J., ed. World's best orations. rev. ed. N. Y., Kaiser, 1923. (Index, v. 10, p. 3971–4107.)

Bryan, William Jennings and Frances Whiting Halsey, ed. World's famous orations. N. Y., Funk and Wagnalls, 1906. (Index, v. 10, p. 263–272.)

Thorndike, Ashley H. Modern eloquence. N. Y., Modern eloquence corp., 1928. (Index, v. 15, p. 175–303.)

Oregon — Economic History
Commonwealth review. Eugene, Oregon, University of Oregon. Index, v. 1–3, Jan. 1916 to July 1918; new series, v. 1–17, April 1919 to Jan. 1936.

Orient
American oriental society journal. New Haven, Conn. Index, v. 1–20, 1843–1899; v. 21–40, 1901–1920.

American schools of oriental research. Bulletin. Philadelphia. General index, no. 1–50, in no. 50, p. 24–26; Topographical index, no. 1–50, p. 26–36; nos. 51–70 in no. 76 p. 15–24; Index to Biblical persons, of ancient oriental rulers, etc., no. 1–70, in no. 74, p. 23–84; Index to articles and archaeological reports, no. 51–80, 1933–1940; List of books and reprints noted in no. 51–80, by Ralph Marcus, in no. 80, p. 28–34.

Ornithology

Auk, a quarterly journal of ornithology. Lancaster, Pa. Index, v. 1–17. 1884–1900; v. 18–27, 1901–1910; v. 28–37, 1911–1920; v. 38–47, 1921–1930.

Bird-lore. N. Y., National assoc. of Audubon societies. Index, v. 1–15, 1899–1913.

Condor. Berkeley, Calif., Cooper ornithological club. Index, v. 1–10, 1899–1908; v. 11–20, 1909–1918; v. 21–30, 1919–1928.

Forest and stream. N. Y. Index to ornithological matter, v. 1–12, 1873–1879.

Nebraska ornithologists' union. Proceedings. Lincoln, Nebraska. Index, v. 1–3, 1899–1902.

Pamphlets

Bennett, Wilma. Occupations and vocational guidance, *see* **Vocations.**

U. S. Office of education. Public affairs pamphlets, *see* **Public Affairs.**

Vertical file service catalog. N. Y., Wilson co., 1932–date.

Willging, Eugene Paul. The index to American Catholic pamphlets, *see* **Catholics.**

Pan American Union

Pan American union. Bulletin. Wash., D. C. Index, v. 27–39, 1908–1914.

Parliamentary Law

Cannon, Clarence. Cannon's Precedents of the House of representatives of the U. S., including references to provisions of the constitution, the laws, and decisions of U. S. Senate. Wash., D. C., Govt. print. off., 1941. Index-digest A-D (v. 9), E-N (v. 10), O-Z (v. 11).

Parties

See also **Games and Dances.**

Lamkin, Nina B. Good times for all times. N. Y., Samuel French, 1929. 377p.

Silk, Agnes K. and Clara E. Fanning, comp. Index to parties. Boston, Faxon, 1930. 121p.

Patents

See also **Trade-Marks and Names.**

Bowman, Border. Indexed digest of patent cases in the U. S. district and circuit courts of appeal, from 1924–1930. N. Y., Baker, Voorhis & co., 1930. 250p.

Kinsev, Victor E. and T. E. Hopkins. Index to iron and steel patents. 2d ed. Pittsburgh, Pa., American compilation co., 1931. 249p.

Patent office society. Journal. Wash., D. C. Index, v. 1–10, 1918–1928; v. 11–20, 1929–1938, by B. M. Federico.

52 AN INDEX TO INDEXES

Randall, Merle and E. B. Watson. Finding list for United States patent, design, trade-mark, reissue, label, print and plant patent numbers. Berkeley, University of California, 1938. 31p.

U. S. Congress. House. Patents committee. Index of reports, 50th — 75th congress, 1888–1938. Wash., D. C., Govt. print. off., 1940, 26p.

U. S. Patent office. Annual report of the Commissioner of patents, 1876–1925. Wash., D. C., Govt. print. off., 1873–1927. (Continued by Index of patents.)

U. S. Patent office. Index of patents issued from the U. S. patent office. Wash., D. C., Govt. print. off. 1920–date. Annual.

U. S. Patent office. Index of patents relating to electricity; granted ... prior to July 1, 1881, with an appendix ... 1881–1882 (annual 1883–1897). Wash., D. C., Govt. print. off.

U. S. Patent office. Official gazette. General index, 1872–1875. Wash., D. C., Govt. print off. 4v. (Continued by Annual report, Index of patents.)

U. S. Patent office. Subject matter index of patents for inventions granted in France, 1791–1796. Wash., D. C., Govt. print. off., 1883. (Also for patents granted to Italy, 1848–1886.)

U. S. Patent office. Subject matter index of patents for inventions issued by the U. S. Patent office from 1790–1873, inclusive. Wash., D. C., Govt. print. off., 1874. 3v.

Worden, Edward C. Chemical patents index. N. Y., Chemical catalog co., inc., 1927–1934. 5v.

Pathology

Chicago pathological society. Transactions. Chicago. Index, v. 1–12, 1894–1927.

Peace

International conciliation. N. Y., Carnegie endowment for international peace. Index, no. 1–325, April 1907–Dec. 1936. Includes Special bulletins, dated but not numbered.

World peace foundation. World peace foundation pamphlets. Boston. Cumulative index, v. 4–6, 1921–1923; v. 7–9, 1924–1926.

Pennsylvania — History

Lancaster Co. Historical society. Historical papers and addresses. Lancaster, Pa. Index to authors whose papers or addresses have appeared in v. 1–35 inclusive, 1896–1932; Index to personal names appearing in v. 11–20, 1906/7–1916; v. 21–26, 1917–1922; v. 27–32, 1923–1928.

Periodicals

See also **Newspapers; Periodicals, General,** Special subjects, i.e. **Accounting.**

AN INDEX TO INDEXES

Abridged Reader's guide to periodical literature, July 1935 to date. Author and subject index to a selected list of periodicals. N. Y., Wilson, 1936–date.

Athenaeum subject index to periodicals, 1915–1916. London, Library association, 1919. 744p. (Later title: Subject index of periodicals.)

Canadian periodical index, see **Canada**.

Catholic periodical index, see **Catholics**.

Cotgreave, Alfred, comp. A contents–subject index to general and periodical literature. London, Stock, 1900. 743p.

Cumulative index to a selected list of periodicals, 1896–1903. Cleveland, O., Cumulative index co., 1897–1903. (Absorbed by Reader's guide in 1903.)

Index to early American periodical literature, 1728–1870. N. Y., New York university, 1940. Indexed by W.P.A. (Order from Pamphlet distributing co., P. O. Box, no. 8 Times square station, N. Y. city.)

*Industrial arts index. Subject index to a selected list of engineering, trade and business periodicals. N. Y., Wilson, 1913–date.

*International index to periodicals, devoted chiefly to the humanities and science. 1907–date. N. Y., Wilson, 1916–date.

*(Annual) Magazine subject index, 1907–date; a subject index to a selected list of American and English periodicals and society publications. Boston, Faxon, 1908–date.

*Poole, William F., ed. An alphabetical index to subjects treated in the reviews and other periodicals to which no indexes have been published. N. Y., Putnam, 1848.

*Poole's index to periodical literature, 1802–1881. rev. ed. Boston, Houghton, 1891. 2v.
Supplements, Jan. 1882–Jan. 1907. 5v.

*Poole's index to periodical literature, 1802–1907. N. Y., Peter Smith, 1938. 6v. in 7. (A reprint of original ed.)

*Poole's index to periodical literature, abridged edition, edited by W. J. Fletcher and Mary Poole. Boston, Houghton, 1901. 843p.
1st supplement, 1900–1904. 260p.

Public affairs information service, see **Public Affairs**.

*Reader's guide to periodical literature. Author and subject index to a selected list of periodicals, 1900–date. N. Y., Wilson, 1900–date.

Review of reviews. Index to the periodicals of 1890–1902, v. 1–13. London and N. Y., Review of reviews, 1891–1903. 13v. Annual.

South African library association. Index to South African periodicals. Pretoria (Box 397), 1940. no. 1–2, Jan.–Je. 1940. Quarterly, to be cumulated annually.

Subject index to the periodicals in science and technology, see **Science**.

Periodicals, General

Atlantic monthly. Boston. Index, v. 1-62, 1857-1888; v. 63-88, 1889-1901.

Eclectic magazine of foreign literature, science and art. N. Y. and Boston. Index, v. 1-96, Ja. 1844-Je. 1881; Index to engravings, 1844-1884; includes index to The Living age, April 1853-Mar. 1881.

Editorial research reports. Wash., D. C. Title index to reports, 1925-1935.

Events. N. Y. Index for the four years, v. 1-8, 1937-1940.

Facts on file. N. Y., Bernard Person. Cumulative indexes, 1941-date.

Forum and century. N. Y. Index, v. 1-32, 1886-1902.

Harper's monthly magazine. N. Y. Index, v. 1-85, 1850-1892.

Harper's weekly. N. Y. Index, v. 1-31, 1857-1887.

Life magazine, *see* **Photographs.**

(Littell's) Living age; weekly. Boston. Index, v. 1-100, 1844-1891.

McBride's magazine. Philadelphia. Index, v. 1-26, 1868-1881.

Mentor. N. Y. The Mentor index, serial no. 1, through no. 192.

Nation. N. Y. Index, v. 1-40, 1865-1885.

New Englander. New Haven, Conn. Index, v. 1-19, 1843-1862 (succeeded by Yale review).

New McClure's magazine. N. Y. Index, v. 1-18, 1893-1902.

New York review. N. Y. Index, v. 1-10, 1837-1842.

North American review. N. Y. Index, v. 1-125, 1815-1877; v. 126-131, 1878-1880.

Partisan review. N. Y. Index, v. 4, 5, and 6, 1937-1939.

Philistine, a periodical of protest. East Aurora, N. Y. Index and concordance, v. 1-20, 1895-1905.

Portfolio. Philadelphia. Index, v. 1-20, 1816-1825.

Scribner's magazine. N. Y. Index, v. 1-10, 1887-1891.

Scribner's monthly. N. Y. Index, v. 1-10, 1870-1875.

*Time, the weekly news-magazine. N. Y., 1923-date. (Annual indexes.)

Yale review. New Haven, Conn. Index, v. 1-19, 1892-1911.

Personnel Work

Cowley, William Harold. The personnel bibliographical index. Columbus, Ohio state university, 1932. 433p.

Petroleum

American association of petroleum geologists. Publications. Tulsa, Okla. Comprehensive index, 1917-1936, by Daisy Winifred Heath.

American gas institute. Proceedings. Easton, Pa. Index, v. 1-10, 1906-1915.

Pharmacology

American pharmaceutical association. Proceedings. Baltimore. Collective index to v. 51–59 of the Proceedings and to v. 1–14 of the Yearbooks ... from 1903–1925 inclusive.

Journal of pharmacology and experimental therapeutics. Baltimore. Index, v. 1–20, 1910–1923 inclusive.

Philately

The American philatelist. Federalsburg, Md. Cumulative index to v. 1–51, 1887–1938, compiled by A.P.S. philatelic index and literature committee.

Philology

See **Language and Languages.**

Philosophy

American philosophical society. Proceedings. Philadelphia. General index, v. 1–50, 1838–1911; v. 51–57, 1912–1935.

American philosophical society. Philadelphia. Serial list of publications. Transactions, 1818–1938 ... Proceedings, 1876–1938 ... Memoirs, 1935–1938 ... Misc. Publications.

American philosophical society. Transactions. Philadelphia. Index, v. 1–n. s. v. 15, 1769–1888. *In* Subject register of papers published in Transactions and proceedings.

Andover review. Boston. Index, v. 1–10, 1884–1888.

Journal of speculative philosophy. St. Louis, Mo. Index, v. 1–15, 1867–1881.

Monist, a quarterly magazine devoted to the philosophy of science. Chicago. Index, v. 1–17, 1890–1907

Open court. Chicago. Index, v. 1–20, 1887–1906.

Philosophical review. N. Y. Index, v. 1–35, 1892–1926.

Philosophical society of Washington. Bulletin Wash., D. C. Index, v. 1–15, 1874–1910.

Photographs

See also **Portraits.**

Current geographical publications. N. Y., American geographical society. Beginning with Oct. 1939 issue, each number will have as a special supplement a classified list of photographs contained in publications received in the A.G.S. library and indexed in its Photograph catalog.

Life. Chicago. Index, v. 1, 1937–date. Annual.

Physics

See also **Astrophysics; Geophysics; Microscopy; Optics.**

Franklin institute. Journal. Philadelphia. General index, v. 1–200, 1826–1925.

Glazebrook, Sir Richard. Dictionary of applied physics. London and N. Y., Macmillan, 1922-23. (v. 5 includes general index.)

Physical review. Lancaster, Pa. General index, 1893-1920.

Reviews of modern physics. N. Y. Cumulative index, v. 1-10, July 1929-Oct. 1938.

Physiology

The American journal of physiology. Baltimore. Index, v. 1-60, 1898-1922, v. 1-90, 1922-1930.

Physiological review. Baltimore. Index, v. 1-15, 1921-1935.

Pictures

See also **Photographs; Portraits.**

Bailey, Liberty Hyde. Standard catalog of horticulture, *see* **Horticulture.**

Booth, Mary Josephine. Index to material on picture study. Boston. Faxon, 1921. 92p.

*Ellis, Jessie Croft. General index to illustrations. Boston, Faxon, 1931. 467p.

*Ellis, Jessie Croft. Nature index; 5000 selected references to nature forms and illustrations of nature in design, painting and sculpture. Boston, Faxon, 1930. 319p.

Ellis, Jessie Croft. Travel through pictures; references to pictures in books and periodicals, of interesting sites all over the world. Boston, Faxon, 1935. 669p.

*Life, *see* **Photographs.**

Mentor. The mentor index, *see* **Periodicals, General.**

Pageant of America. *See* **History**

Shepard, Frederick J Index to illustrations. Chicago, A.L.A., 1924. 89p.

Plays

See **Drama.**

Poetry

See also **Children's Poetry; Quotations.**

*Bruncken, Herbert. Subject index to poetry; a guide for adult readers. Chicago, A.L.A., 1940. 201p.

*Granger, Edith. Index to poetry and recitations. 3d ed., rev. and enl. Chicago, McClurg, 1940. 1525p.

Poet lore. Boston. Index, v. 1-25, 1889-1914.

Whitman, Charles H. Subject index to the poems of Edmund Spenser. New Haven, Conn., Conn. academy of arts and sciences, Yale university press, 1918. 261p.

Political Science

See also **International Law and Relations; Public Affairs; U. S. Foreign Relations.**

American academy of political and social science. The Annals. *See* **Sociology.**

American political science review. Baltimore. General index, v. 1–20, 1906–1926, and to the Proceedings of the American political science association, 1904–1914.

Political science quarterly. N. Y. and Boston, Academy of political science. Index, v. 1–35, 1886–1930.

Population

Population index. Princeton, N. J., School of public affairs, Princeton university and the Population association of America. v. 1–6, 1935–1940.

Portraits

*A.L.A. portrait index; index to portraits contained in printed books and periodicals, edited by W. C. Lane and N. E. Browne. Wash., D. C., Govt. print. off., 1906. 1600p.

Life magazine, *see* **Photographs.**

Wheatley, Henry B. Portraits in books. *In* Bibliographical society transactions, 1896–1898, p. 129–136.

Postage Stamps
See **Philately.**

Pottery
See **Ceramics.**

Prices

See also **Books — Prices.**

Shively, Eva T. Index to some sources of current prices. (Bibliographical contributions 5.) Wash., D. C., Govt. print. off., 1923. 124p.

U. S. Dept. of commerce. Price sources, index of commercial and economic publications currently received in the libraries of the Dept. of commerce which contain current market commodity prices. Compiled by Elizabeth M. Carmack. Wash., D. C., Govt. print. off., 1931. 324p.

Prisons

American prison association. Proceedings of the annual congress of the American prison association. Index, 1905–1934. Wash., D. C., U. S. Bureau of prisons, Dept. of justice, 1936. 320p.

Journal of prison discipline and philanthropy. Philadelphia, Penn. prison society. Index, v. 1–10, 1845–1855.

Proverbs
See **Quotations**.

Psychology
See also **Tests, Mental**.

American journal of psychology. Ithaca, N. Y., Cornell university. Index, v. 1-30, 1887-1919.

The psychoanalytic review. Wash., D. C., Subject-author index, v. 1-18, 1913-1931.

Psychological abstracts, 1927-date. Lancaster, Pa., American psychological association, 1927-date. Subject and author indexes.

Psychological index, 1894-date. Princeton, N. J., Psychological review co., 1894-date.

Rickmann, John, comp. Index psychoanalyticus. London, Hogarth press-institute of psychoanalysis, 1928. 276p. (Covers 1893-1926.)

Public Affairs
*Public affairs information service. N. Y., Public affairs inf. service, 1915-date.

U. S. Office of education. Public affairs pamphlets; an index to inexpensive pamphlets on social, economic, political and international affairs. (Bulletin of education bulletin 1937, no. 3.) Wash., D. C., Govt. print. off., 1937. 85p.

Supplement, no. 1 (Bulletin 1937, no. 3, supp. no. 1). 1938. 66p.

Public Health
See **Hygiene and Public Health**.

Quotations
See also **Law — Maxims**.

Allibone, Samuel Austin. Great authors of all ages. Philadelphia, Lippincott, 1891. 555p.

Allibone, Samuel Austin. Poetical quotations from Chaucer to Tennyson. Philadelphia, Lippincott, 1891. 788p.

Allibone, Samuel Austin. Prose quotations from Socrates to Macaulay. Phil., Lippincott, 1889. 764p.

Apperson, G. L. English proverbs and proverbial phrases, a historical dictionary. London, Dent; N. Y., Dutton, 1929. 721p.

*Bartlett, John. Familiar quotations, edited by Christopher Morley and Louella D. Everett. 11th ed., rev. and enl. Boston, Little Brown, 1937. 1578p.

Belton, John Devoe. Literary manual of foreign phrases and classical quotations, ancient and modern. N. Y., Putnam, 1891. 249p.

Benham, William. Benham's book of quotations, proverbs and household words. rev. ed. London, Ward, Lock, 1929. 1226p. (An American edition, with title Putnam's complete quotations, is also published.)

AN INDEX TO INDEXES

Benham, William. Cassell's classified quotations from authors of all nations and periods grouped under subject-headings, with full index of cross references. London, Cassell, 1921. 653p.

Bent, Samuel Arthur. Familiar short sayings of great men; with historical and explanatory notes. 9th ed., rev. and enl. Boston, Houghton, 1896. 665p.

Bohn, Henry George. Handbook of proverbs. London, Bell, 1889. 583p.

Bohn, Henry George. Polyglot of foreign proverbs. London, Bell, 1889. 579p.

Champion, Selwyn Gurney. Racial proverbs. N. Y., Macmillan, 1938. 767p.

Christy, Robert. Proverbs, maxims and phrases of all ages. N. Y., Putnam, 1905. 2v. in 1.

Dalbiac, Lilian. Dictionary of quotations (German) with authors' and subjects' indexes. London, Sonnenschein; N. Y., Macmillan, 1906. 485p.

Dalbiac, Philip Hugh. Dictionary of quotations (English) with author and subject indexes. London, Sonnenschein; N. Y., Macmillan, 1908. 544p.

Day, Edward Parsons. Day's collacon; an encyclopedia of prose quotations, with biographical index of authors. London, Low, 1883. 1216p.

Dictionary of best known quotations and proverbs, edited by Ernest Rhys. N. Y., Garden City, 1939. 2v. in 1. (200-page subject and keyword index.)

Douglas, Charles Noel. Forty thousand quotations, prose and poetical ... from the standard authors of ancient and modern times, classified according to subject. N. Y., Sully, 1915. 2000p.

Durfee, Charles A. Concise poetical concordance to the principal poets of the world. N. Y., Alden, 1894. 639p.

Edwards, Tryon. Dictionary of thoughts; a cyclopedia of laconic quotations. N. Y., Cassell, 1891. 644p.

Harbottle, Thomas Benfield. Dictionary of quotations (classical). London, Sonnenschein, 1897. 648p.

Harbottle, Thomas Benfield, and Philip Hugh Dalbiac. Dictionary of quotations (French and Italian). London, Sonnenschein; N. Y., Macmillan, 1901. 565p.

Harbottle, Thomas Benfield and Philip Hugh Dalbiac. Dictionary of quotations, Italian. London, Sonnenschein; N. Y., Macmillan, 1909. (A reprint of the Italian section of their Dictionary of quotations, French and Italian.)

Harbottle, Thomas Benfield. Dictionary of quotations, Latin. London, Sonnenschein; N. Y., Macmillan, 1909. 389p. (A reprint of the Latin section of his Dictionary of quotations, Classical, with an appendix of additional material.)

Hazlitt, William Carew. English proverbs and proverbial phrases. N. Y., Scribner, 1907. 580p.

Hoyt, Jehiel Keeler. Hoyt's new encyclopedia of practical quotations, edited by Kate Louise Roberts. N. Y., Funk, 1922–1940. 1345p.

Jones, Hugh Percy. Dictionary of foreign phrases and classical quotations with English translations or equivalents. London, Deacon; Philadelphia, Lippincott, 1900. 532p.

King, William Francis Henry. Classical and foreign quotations; a polyglot manual of historical and literary sayings, noted passages in poetry and prose, phrases, proverbs, and bon-mots, compiled, edited, and told with references, translations and indexes. 3d ed., rev. and rewritten. London, Whitaker, 1904. 412p.

Latham, Edward. Famous sayings and their authors; a collection of historical sayings in French, English, German, Greek, Italian and Latin. London, Sonnenschein; N. Y., Dutton, 1904. 269p.

Lean, Vincent Stuckey. Lean's collectanea. London, Simpkin, 1902–1904. 4v. in 5.

Marvin, Dwight Edwards. Curiosities in proverbs. N. Y., Putnam, 1916. 428p.

Marvin, Frederic Rowland. The last words, real and traditional of distinguished men and women, collected from various sources. N. Y., Revell, 1901. 336p.

Mead, Levon and F. N. Gilbert. Manual of forensic quotations. N. Y., Taylor, 1903. 207p.

Moritz, Robert Edward. Memorabilia mathematica, or Philomath's quotations book. London and N. Y., Macmillan, 1914. 410p.

Ramage, Craufurd Tait. Beautiful thoughts from French and Italian translations. 4th ed. London, Routledge, 1884. 619p.

Ramage, Craufurd Tait. Beautiful thoughts from German and Spanish authors. new rev. ed. London, Routledge, 1884. 559p.

Ramage, Craufurd Tait. Beautiful thoughts from Greek authors, with English translations. London, Routledge, 1895. 589p.

Ramage, Craufurd Tait. Beautiful thoughts from Latin authors, with English translations. London, Routledge, 1895. 855p.

Riley, Henry Thomas. Dictionary of Latin and Greek quotations, proverbs, maxims, and mottoes, classical and medieval. London, Bell, 1888. 622p.

Scarborough, William. Collection of Chinese proverbs. Shanghai, Presbyterian mission press, 1926. 381p.

Smith, William G. Oxford dictionary of English proverbs. Oxford, Clarendon press, 1935. 644p.

*Stevenson, Burton Egbert. Home book of quotations, classical and modern. 3d ed., rev. and enl. N. Y., Dodd, 1937. 2811p.

Stevenson, Burton Egbert. The home book of Shakespeare quotations. N. Y., Scribner, 1937. 2055p.

Swan, Helena. Dictionary of contemporary quotations (English). London, Sonnenschein; N. Y., Dutton, 1904. 608p.

Taylor, Archer. The proverb. Cambridge, Mass., Harvard univ. press, 1931. 223p.

Treffry, Elford E. Stokes' encyclopedia of familiar quotations, containing five thousand selections from six hundred authors. N. Y., Stokes; London, Chambers, 1906. 763p.

Wale, William. What great men have said about great men. London, Sonnenschein; N. Y., Dutton, 1902. 482p.

Walsh, Richard Shepard. International encyclopedia of prose and poetical quotations from the literature of the world. new ed. Phil., Winston, 1931. 1029p.

Wilstach, Frank Jenners. Dictionary of similes. new ed., rev. and enl. Boston, Little, 1924. 578p.

Wood, James. Nuttall dictionary of quotations from ancient and modern, English and foreign sources . . . new ed., with supplement of over 1000 quotations including many from modern authors, compiled by H. L. Hayden. London and N. Y., Warne, 1930. 659p.

Radio

Radio daily. N. Y. The radio annual, 1938– . N.Y., Radio daily, 1938–date. (Index in front.)

Radio Engineering

Institute of radio engineers. Proceedings. N. Y. Index, 1909–1936, inclusive.

Radio Forums

Town meeting; bulletin of America's town meeting of the air. N.Y., Index, v. 1–5, 1935–1939.

Railroads

U. S. Railroad labor board. Decisions. Cumulative index to decisions. to Jan. 1, 1925, including a cumulative index to regulations . . . v. 1–5, inclusive. Decisions, nos. 1–2773. Wash., D. C., Govt. print. off., 1925. 188p. (Printed as a supplement to v. 5, 1924.)

Railways
See **Transportation.**

Readers

Lynch, Abigail, comp. Classified index of materials contained in different series of school readers. San Francisco, Alexander Dulfer ptg. co., 1910, 71p.

Rue, Eloise, comp. Subject index to books for intermediate grades. Chicago, A.L.A., 1940. 495p.

Rue, Eloise, comp. Subject index to readers. Chicago, A.L.A., 1938. 174p.

Readings and Recitations
See also **Drama; Monologs; Poetry.**
Ohr, Elizabeth, comp. Stories and poems for opening exercises, *see* **Children's Literature.**
*Silk, Agnes K. and Clara E. Fanning. Index to dramatic readings. Boston, Faxon, 1925. 303p.

Reclamation
See **Soils.**

Reference Books
Minto, John, ed. Reference books; a classified and annotated guide to the principal works of reference... London, Library assoc., 1929. 356p.
Supplement to reference books. London, Library assoc., 1931. 140p.
Mudge, Isadore G. Guide to reference books. 6th ed. Chicago, A.L.A., 1936. 504p.
Reference books of 1935–1937. Chicago, A.L.A., 1939. 90p. (Followed by Winchell's Reference books of 1938–40.)
Shores, Louis. Basic reference books. 2d ed. Chicago, A.L.A., 1939. 486p.
Wilcox, Jerome Kear. U. S. reference publications, *see* **Government Documents.**
Winchell, Constance M. Reference books of 1938–40. Second informal supplement to Guide to reference books... Chicago, A.L.A., 1941. 106p.

Refrigeration
American society of refrigerating engineers. Transactions. N. Y. Thirty year index. *In* Refrigerating engineering 28:331–54, Dec. 1934.

Religion
See also **Catholics; Ethics; Friends, Society of; Jews.**
American journal of theology. Chicago. Index, v. 1–24, 1897–1920.
Anglican theological review. Evanston, Ill. Index, v. 1–10, 1918–1927; v. 11–20, 1928–1938.
Biblical world. Chicago. Index, v. 1–28, 1882–1906.
Bibliotheca sacra, a religious and sociological quarterly. Andover, Mass. Index, v. 1–30, 1844–1874.
Chandler, Frank R., ed. Indexes to the Bible. Chicago, The Editor, 744 Rush st. 75p. (Issued in connection with 20th century edition of King James version.)
Christian examiner. Boston. Index, v. 1–87, 1824–1869.

AN INDEX TO INDEXES

Congregational quarterly. Boston. Index, v. 1–10, 1859–1868; v. 11–20, 1869–1878.
Ecclesiastical review. Philadelphia. Index, v. 1–50, Jan. 1889–June 1914.
Harvard theological review. Cambridge, Mass. Index, v. 1–30, 1908–1937.
Harvard university. Harvard-Yenching institute. Combined indices to the authors and titles of books and chapters in four collections of Buddhistic literature. Cambridge, Harvard univ. press, 1933. 3v.
Hastings, James. Dictionary of the Bible. N. Y., Scribner, 1898–1902. (v. 5 contains index.)
*Hastings, James, ed. Encyclopedia of religion and ethics. N. Y., Scribners, 1927. (Index, volume 13.)
Homiletic review. N. Y. Comprehensive index, v. 1–30, 1876–1895; v. 31–42, 1896–1901.
Methodist review. N. Y. Index, by Elijah H. Pilcher, 1818–1881.
Religious education association. An index to all the publications of the Religious education from Feb. 1903 to Feb. 1912. Chicago, Religious educ. assoc., 1912. 40p.
Richardson, Ernest Cushing. An alphabetical subject index and index encyclopedia of periodical articles on religion, 1890–1899. N. Y., Scribner, 1907–1911. 2v.
Richardson, Ernest Cushing. Periodical articles on religion, 1890–1899; author index. N. Y., Scribner, 1911. 876p.
Treasury. N. Y. Index, v. 1–13, 1883–1896.
Universalist quarterly and general review. Boston, Index, v. 1–48, 1844–1891.

Rubber
Rubber chemistry and technology, *see* **Chemistry**.

Saints
Baring-Gould, Sabine. Lives of the saints. Edinburg, Grant, 1914. 16v. (v. 16 includes indices.)

Salesmanship
Printed salesmanship. Cambridge, Mass. Six year index, v. 50, no. 2–61, October 1927–August 1933.

Scholarship
See **Dissertations; Education; Humanities; Universities and Colleges.**

Science
See also Names of sciences, i.e. **Anthropology; Chemistry**, etc.
Academy of natural sciences of Philadelphia. Phil. Index to scientific contents of the journal and proceedings of the Academy, 1817–1910; edited by Edward J. Nolan.

Academy of science of St. Louis. Transactions. Index, v. 1–14, 1856/60–1905.
American journal of science. New Haven, Conn. Index, v. 1–49, 1818–1869. (With every series every 10th volume includes an index which covers preceding 10 vols. Since v. 50, then indexes issued every five years bound in v. 60, 70, 80, 90, 100, 110, 120.)
Davenport academy of science. Proceedings. Davenport, Iowa. Index, v. 1–5, 1867/76–1885/89.
Denison university. Scientific laboratories. Granville, O. Index, v. 1–10, 1885–1897.
Elisha Mitchell scientific society. Journal. Chapel Hill, N. C. Index, v. 1–31, 1883/84–1916; v. 32–37, 1916–1922; v. 38–44, 1922–1929.
Illinois state academy of science. Transactions. Springfield, Ill. General index, v. 1–25, 1908–1932, compiled by Dorothy E. Rose.
Indiana academy of science. Proceedings. Indianapolis, Ind. Index, 1891–1900.
International catalogue of scientific literature, 1st–14th issues. Published for the International council. London, Royal society of London, 1902–1919.
National academy of sciences. Publications of the National academy of sciences of the U. S. of America, 1915–1926; Part I — Index to the first ten vols. of the Proceedings, 1915–1924; Part II — List of other publications by the Academy from 1863–1920; Part III — List of publications of the N.R.C. from 1916–1925. Easton, Pa.
National research council. Bulletin. Wash., D. C. Index, v. 1–10, 1919–1925.
National research council. International critical tables of numerical data of physics, chemistry, and technology prepared under auspices of the council and the National academy of sciences, edited by Edward Washburn and others. N. Y., McGraw, 1926–1933. (Index, v. 8.)
New York academy of science. Transactions. N. Y. Index, v. 1–15, 1881–1896.
Oklahoma academy of science. Proceedings. Norman, Oklahoma. Index, v. 1–10, 1921–1930. *In* Univ. of Oklahoma Bulletin, n.s., no. 525.
Popular science monthly. N. Y. Index, v. 1–40, 1872–1892.
Scientific American supplement. N. Y. Index, v. 1–70, 1876–1910.
Subject index to the periodicals in science and technology, 1915–1922. 1926–date. London, Library assoc., 1919–date.

Scotland
Stuart, Margaret. Scottish family history, *see* **Genealogy**.

Selective Service
U. S. Selective service system. Index to selective service law, regulations and forms. Wash., D. C., Govt. print. off., 1940. 34p. (Covers 6 volumes of selective service regulations.)

Sequels
See **Series, Books in.**

Series, Books in
Aldred, Thomas. Sequel stories, English and American. 2d ed., by W. H. Parker. London, Assoc. of Assistant librarians, 1928. 91p.

Wead, Katherine H. List of series and sequels for juvenile readers. new and rev. Boston, Faxon, 1923. 63p.

Sewage
Sewage works journal. Lancaster, Pa. Nine-year index, v. 1–9, 1929–1937.

Shakespeare, William
Stevenson, Burton E. The home book of Shakespeare quotations, see **Quotations.**

Short Stories
See also **Children's Literature; Fairy Tales.**

*Firkins, Ina Ten Eyck. Index to short stories. 2d and enl. ed. N. Y., Wilson, 1923. 573p.
First supplement, 1929.
Second supplement, 1936.
(New revised edition in preparation.)

Hannigan, Francis J., comp. Standard index to short stories, 1900–1914. Boston, Snall, 1918. 334p.

Morgan, Vera E. Vocations in short stories, see **Vocations.**

Salisbury, Grace E. and M. E. Beckwith. Index to short stories, see **Children's Literature.**

Smithsonian Institution
See also **Mining and Metallurgy.**

Smithsonian institution. Catalogue of publications, 1846–1882, with an alphabetical index. (Smithsonian misc. collections, v. 27, no. 478.) Wash., D. C., Govt. print. off., 1882. 328p.

Social Hygiene
Journal of social hygiene. N. Y. Index, v. 1–21, 1914–1936. ("Journal of social hygiene as permanent reference material.")

Social Service
Charities review. N. Y. Index, v. 1–8, 1891–1898.

National conference of charities. Proceedings. Fort Wayne, Ind. Cumulative index, v. 1–33, 1874–1906. 4pts. in 1v.

National conference of social work. Proceedings. Chicago, University of Chicago press. Index, v. 1–60, 1874–1933.

Social service review. Chicago. Index, v. 1–10, 1927–1936.

Sociology

*American academy of political and social science. The Annals. Phil. Index, 1890–1915 (25th anniversary index); 1916–1921; 1921–1926 (35th anniversary index); 1926–1930; 1931–1935 (45th anniversary index), 1936–1940.

*American journal of sociology. Chicago. Classified index, v. 1–40, 1895–1935.

American sociological society. Papers. Baton Rouge, La. Index to the sociological papers and reports... 1906–1930, prepared by W. P. Meroney. *In* v. 25, 1930, p. 226–258. (Includes papers presented before the Society which have been published elsewhere.)

*Encyclopedia of the social sciences. N. Y., Macmillan, 1937. (Index, v. 1–5.)

Newark, N. J. Library. Subject index to about 500 societies which issue publications relating to social questions. N. Y., Wilson, 1915. 20p.

Social science abstracts. Index to v. 1–4, 1929–1932. N. Y., Social Science abstracts, inc., Columbia university. (Annual indexes.)

Soils

Soil science. New Brunswick, N. J. Index, authors and subjects, v. 1–25, 1916–1928, compiled by J. S. Joffe, assisted by Herminie B. Kitchen.

U. S. Bureau of agricultural chemistry. Index of publications of Bureau ..., 75 years, 1862–1937; v. 1 List of titles and authors, prepared by H. P. Holman and others. Wash., D. C., Govt. print. off., 1939. 546p.

U. S. Bureau of reclamation. Index to 1st–20th Annual reports. *In* 20th annual report, 1920–1921, p. 583–642. Wash., D. C., Govt. print. off., 1921.

Soldiers, Revolutionary

See **Genealogy.**

Songs

See also **Ballads; Children's Songs; Hymns.**

*Sears, Minnie Earl and Phyllis Crawford. Song index, an index to more than 12,000 songs in 177 collections. N. Y., Wilson, 1926. 650p. Supplement. 1934. 367p.

South — History

See also **Southwest;** Names of southern states, i.e. **Virginia.**

Southern historical society. Papers. Richmond, Virginia state library. Author and subject index, v. 1–38, 1876–1913, by K. P. Minor. *In* Virginia state library Bulletin, v. 6, no. 3–4.

South Dakota — History

South Dakota historical collections. Pierre, S. D. Index, v. 1–16, 1902–1935, compiled by Ethel Collins Jacobsen.

Southwest

Southwest review. Dallas, Texas. Index, v. 10–21, 1924–1936, compiled by Lois Bailey. (Issued as supplement to v. 21, no. 4, July 1936.)

Spanish Language

Hispania. Palo Alto, California, Stanford University. Index, v. 1–5, 1918–1922; v. 6–10, 1923–1927; v. 11–20, 1928–1937.

Special Collections

American historical association. Union list of collections, see **History**.

American library directory... compiled by Bertine E. Weston. N. Y., Bowker, 1939. 531p. (Index, p. 521–531.)

Johnston, William Dawson and Isadore G. Mudge. Special collections in libraries in the U. S. (Office of education bulletin 1912, no. 23.) Wash., D. C., Govt. print. off., 1912. 140p.

Ohio state archaeological and historical society. An index and list of pamphlets collected by Rutherford Birchard Hayes, 19th president of the U. S. Fremont, Ohio, Hayes memorial library, Spiegel Grove State park, 1935. 45p.

Richardson, Ernest Cushing. An index directory to special collections in North American libraries. Yardley, Pa., Cook, 1927. 168p.

Special libraries directory of the United States and Canada, compiled by Special libraries association, special committee; Eleanor S. Cavanaugh, chairman. N. Y., Special libraries assoc., 1935. 253p.

Special library resources, edited by Rose L. Vormelker. v. 1, United States and Canada. N. Y., Special libraries assoc., 1941. 764p.

Winchell, Constance M. Locating books for interlibrary loan; with a bibliography of printed aids which show location of books in American libraries. N. Y., Wilson, 1930. 170p.

Spectroscopy

American society for testing materials. Index to the literature on spectrochemical analysis, see **Chemistry**.

Tuckerman, Alfred. Index to the literature of the spectroscope, 1887–1900. Wash., D. C., Smithsonian institution, 1902. (Continuation of the previous index by the same author published in 1888.) 373p.

Speech

See also **Debate; Orations.**

National speech arts assoc. Proceedings. N. Y., Index to first 16 annual reports in 16th annual convention. 1893–1906, 1907, p. 237–245.

Speaker; a quarterly magazine. N. Y. Index, v. 1–32, 1905–1913.

*Sutton, Roberta Briggs. Speech index. N. Y., Wilson, 1935. 272p.

Thonssen, Elizabeth Fatherson, comp. Bibliography of speech education. N. Y., Wilson, 1939. 800p. (Annotated index of speech materials in English language.)

Standards

See also **Engineering.**

U. S. Bureau of standards. Alphabetical index and numerical list of federal specifications promulgated by the Federal specifications board, complete to Nov. 1, 1929. (Circular no. 378.) Wash., D. C., Govt. print. off., 1929.

U. S. Bureau of standards. Publications, 1901–1925 (list and index). (Circular no. 24.) Wash., D. C., Govt. print. off., 1925. 271p.

U. S. Bureau of Standards. Supplementary list (with index) of the publications of the Bureau of standards, July 1, 1925 to Dec. 31, 1931. Wash., D. C., Govt. print. off., 1932. 214p.

Statistics

See also Special subjects, i.e. **Agriculture; Labor.**

American statistical association. Journal. Wash., D. C., Index, v. 1–34, 1888–1939, prepared by Myron S. Heidingsfield and Harold R. Hosea, consultant.

Annals of mathematical statistics. Baltimore, Md. Cumulative index, v. 1–10, 1930–1939.

Statistics on Canadian commodities. N. Y., Special libraries assoc., 1935. sheet.

Statistics on commodities. N. Y., Special libraries assoc., 1931. sheet.

Tariff

U. S. Tariff commission. Subject index of Tariff publications, revised 1934, with supplements in 1936 and Jan. 1939. Wash., D. C., Govt. print. off., 1934–1939. (Covers period since 1917.)

Technology

See also **Engineering; Science,** etc.

Industrial arts index, *see* **Periodicals.**

Pittsburgh. Carnegie library. Index to subject catalog of the technology department. Pittsburgh, Carnegie library, 1909. 50p.

Pittsburgh. Carnegie library. Technical book review index, issued by the Technology department of the Carnegie library of Pittsburgh. Pittsburgh, Carnegie library, 1917–1929. 12v.

Subject index to the periodicals in science and technology, *see* **Science.**

Technical book review index, 1935/37–date. N. Y., Special libraries Assoc., 1935/37, monthly. (Continues informally, with a gap of some 7 years, the Pittsburgh, Carnegie library index.)

Telegraph and Telephone

Bell laboratories record. N. Y. Index, v. 1-7, 1925-1929; v. 8-12, Sept. 1929-1934.

Bell system technical journal. N. Y. Table of contents and index, v. 1-10, 1922-1931.

Tests, Mental

Educational, psychological and personality tests, by Oscar K. Buros. (Rutgers univ. studies in education.) New Brunswick, N. J., School of education, Rutgers univ., 1933, 1934 and 1935, 83p; 1936, 141p.

Hildreth, Gertrude H. A bibliography of mental tests and rating scales. N. Y., Psychological corporation, 1939. 295p.

Mental measurements yearbook, Oscar K. Buros, editor. Highland Park, N. J., Mental measurements yearbook. 1938, 1940, 1941 and every 2 years hereafter. (Includes periodicals directory and index, Publishers directory and index, Index of titles, Index of names.)

South, Earl Bennett. An index of periodical literature on testing, 1921-1936. N. Y., Psychological corporation, 1937. 286p.

Wang, Charles K. A. An annotated bibliography of mental tests and scales. Peiping, China, Catholic university press, 1939. 2v.

Theatre

See also **Drama.**

Billboard. Cincinnati. Annual index.

Theology

See **Religion.**

Trade Marks and Names

Amos, Alice M. Where to find the new trade names. Technical library, Edgewood Arsenal, 1940. 32p.

Special libraries association. Trade names index. N. Y., Special libraries association, 1941. 178p.

U. S. Patent office. Index of trade-marks issued from U. S. Patent office. Wash., D. C., Govt. print. off. Annual index.

Transportation

See also **Aeronautics; Highways; Railroads.**

American railway bridge and building association, *see* **Engineering.**

American railway master mechanics' association. Report of proceedings. Chicago. Index, v. 1-33, 1868-1900.

American transit association. Summary index of Proceedings of the A.T.A., v. 1-52, 1882-1934; American transit accountants' association, v. 1-37, 1897-1934; American transit claims association, v. 6-29, 1906-1934; American transit operating association, v. 1-26, 1908-1934, and their predecessors. N. Y., A.T.A., 1935. 95p.

American transit engineering association. Proceedings. N. Y. Index, v. 1-31, 1903-1933.

Electric railway journal. N. Y. Index, v. 1-22, 1884-1903.

Street railway journal. N. Y. General index, by subjects and authors, v. 1-22, Oct. 1884-Dec. 1903.

Transit journal. N. Y. Index, v. 1-22, 1884-1903.

Travel
See also **Geography.**

Ellis, Jessie Croft. Travel through pictures, *see* **Pictures.**

Treaties
League of Nations. Treaty series. General indexes, *see* **League of Nations.**

U. S. Dept. of state. Treaty information. Cumulative index, Bulletins 1-69 inclusive, Oct. 1929-June 1935; Bulletins 70-116 inclusive, July 1935-June 1939. Wash., D. C., Govt. print. off., 1937, 133p.; 1940, 92p.

Trusts
Trust bulletin. N. Y. Cumulative index, v. 15-19, Sept.1935-August 1940.

Trust companies. N. Y. Five year cumulative index of articles, surveys and other news and discussion relating to fiduciary matters (including legal decisions) appearing in Trust companies magazine, v. 52-61, Jan. 1931-Dec. 1935. *In* June issue, 1936, p. 129-160.

U. S. Congress
*Congressional record. Wash., D. C., Govt. print. off. Annual index.

Ordway, Albert. General index of the Journals of congress, 1st-16th, inclusive, being a synoptical subject index of the proceedings on all public business, 1789-1821 with reference to debates, documents and statutes, 1880-1883. (Serial no. 1939, 2071.) Wash., D. C., Govt. print. off. 2v.

Ordway, Albert. General personal index of Journals of congress, 1st-16th, being an index to personal record of members of Congress, 1789-1821. (Serial no. 2331, 2446.) Wash., D. C., Govt. print. off., 2v.

U. S. Congress. House. Congressional committee hearings. An index to those prior to Jan. 3, 1939 in the Library of the U. S. House of representatives. Wash., D. C., Govt. print. off., 1939. 609p.

U. S. Congress. House. General personal index of the Journals of congress, 1880-1883. (House reports, 46th congress, 2d sess., no. 1776; 47th congress, 1st sess., no. 1559). Wash., D. C., Govt. print. off.

U. S. Congress. House. Index to the executive communications made to the House, and Index to the reports of committees. Wash., D. C., Govt. print. off., 1824-1870. Issued from time to time. (Together for 1789-1839 and separately for 1839-1869. 6pts. In Congressional series.)

AN INDEX TO INDEXES 71

U. S. Congress. Senate. Index to Congressional committee hearings (not confidential in character) prior to Jan. 3, 1935, in the U. S. Senate. Wash., D. C., Govt. print. off., 1927. 1056p.
Supplement, Jan. 3, 1935–Jan. 3, 1939. 270p.

U. S. Foreign Relations

See also International Law and Relations; Public Affairs; Tariff; Treaties.

American foreign service journal. Wash., D. C. Index, v. 1–5, 1924–1928.

U. S. Dept. of state. General index to the published volumes of the diplomatic correspondence and foreign relations of the U. S., 1861–1899. Wash., D. C., Govt. print. off., 1902. 945p.

Units of Work

Carey, Alice E., Paul Hanna and J. L. Meriam. Catalog, units of work, activities, projects, etc. N. Y., Teachers college, Columbia university, 1932. 290p.

Universities and Colleges

American assoc. of collegiate registrars. Journal. Philadelphia. Index of Proceedings of the Association from 1910–1925; Bulletin of the Assoc., v. 1–12, by Wilbur Keeling. *In* the Journal, v. 13, p. 115–145.

American association of teachers colleges. Yearbooks. Indexes to yearbooks of teachers colleges, 1922–1937. *In* Yearbook 1938, p. 170–190.

American association of university professors. Bulletin. Easton, Pa. Index, v. 1–10, July 1915–Dec. 1924; v. 11–20, 1925–1934.

Brahm, Walter Thomas. Bibliography and index of publications of Western Reserve university for the years 1822–1936. Cleveland, Western Reserve University, 1937. 83p.

Colorado. University. University of Colorado studies. Boulder, Colo. Contents and author-index, v. 1–25, 1902–1938.

Harvard graduates' magazine. Boston. Index, v. 1–20, 1892–1912.

Kansas university quarterly. Lawrence, Kansas. Index, v. 1–10, 1892–1901.

North Dakota university. Quarterly journal. University, N. D. Index, v. 15, 1910–1925.

Princeton review. N. Y. Index, v. 1–4, n s v. 1–40, 1825–1868.

Tauber, Maurice F. Index of theses and dissertations prepared at Temple university library. Philadelphia, Temple university library, 1935. 44p.

Teachers college, Columbia university. Teachers college bulletin. N. Y. Register of doctoral dissertations, v. 1, 1899–1936. (28 series, no. 4, Feb. 1936.)

Tonne, Herbert Arthur. List of doctors' and masters' theses in education, New York university, 1890–June 1936. Rho chapter, Phi Delta Kappa, School of education, N. Y. university, N. Y., 1937. 117p.

University review; a journal of the University of Kansas City. Kansas City, Mo. Index, v. 1-5, 1934-1939.

Washington university. Studies. St. Louis, Mo. Contents-index, v. 1-10, 1913-1923.

Wyoming. University. Publications. Index, v. 1-6, June 15, 1922-Feb. 15, 1939, by Reta Ridings.

Veterinary Zoology
See Zoology.

Virginia — History
Swem, Earl G. Virginia historical index. Roanoke, Va., Stone printing and manuf. co., 1934-1935. 2v. 1118p.; 1181p.

Visual Aids
See also Motion Pictures; Pictures.

Wheeling, Katherine and Jane A. Hilson. Illustrative material for junior and senior high school literature. N. Y., Wilson, 1930. 80p.

Vocational Education
Gray, Rolland O. and William L. Hunter. Index to 2500 books on industrial arts education and vocational industrial education, 1820-1934. Ames, Ia., Iowa state college, 1935. 108p.

Hunter, William L. and E. G. Livingston. Guide to magazine articles on industrial arts education and vocation industrial education. Ames, Ia., Iowa state college, 1934. 75p.

Vocations
See also Personnel Work; Vocational Education.

Allen, Frederick J. A guide to the study of occupations; a selected critical bibliography of the common occupations with specific references for their study. Cambridge, Mass., Harvard univ. press. 1925. 197p.

Bennett, Wilma. Occupations and vocational guidance, a source list of pamphlet material. 3d ed. N. Y., Wilson, 1938. 102p.

Gilpatrick, Edward M. An index to occupations. References to a bibliography containing job analyses of the specific occupations listed. *In* Vocational guidance magazine 11:78-94, Nov. 1932.

Index to occupations. Fort Wayne, Indiana, Public library of Fort Wayne and Allen co., 1936. 111p.

*Lingenfelter, Mary R. Vocations in fiction. 2d ed. Chicago, A.L.A., 1938. 99p.

Morgan, Vera E. Vocations in short stories. Chicago, A.L.A., 1938. 47p.

National occupational conference. Occupational index. N. Y., Wilson, 1936-date.

AN INDEX TO INDEXES

Parker, Willard E. Books about jobs, a bibliography of occupational literature. Chicago, National occupational conference, 1936. (Index, p. 395–402.)

*Price, Willodeen and Zelma E. Ticen, comp. Index to vocations. 2d ed. N. Y., Wilson, 1938. 122p.

U. S. Bureau of census. Alphabetical index of occupations and industries. 16th census of the U. S. Wash., D. C., Govt. print. off., 1940. 607p.

Vocational guide. Chicago, Science research associates. Dec. 1938–date.

Vocational index to Fortune. N. Y., Lecturer's bureau of Time–Life–Fortune, 1941. 44p.

Water

American water works association. Index to the Proceedings, Journal, and other publications of the Assoc., 1881–1939 inclusive. N. Y., The Assoc., 1940. 281p.

New England water works assoc. Index to the Transactions and Journal, 1882–1931. Transactions, 1883–1885. Journal, v. 1–44, 1886–1930. Boston, Fort Hill press, Usher, 1931. 44p. (Issued as v. 45, no. 2, p. 2 of the Journal.)

U. S. Geological survey. Bibliographic review and index of papers relating to under-ground water, published by the U. S. Geological survey, 1879–1904, by M. L. Fuller. (Water supply paper 120.) Wash., D. C., Govt. print. off., 1905. 128p.

U. S. Geological survey. Bibliographic review and index of underground water literature published in the U. S. in 1905 by M. L. Fuller and others. (Water supply paper 163.) Wash., D. C., Govt. print. off., 1906. 130p.

U. S. Geological survey. Bibliography and index of publications to U. S. Geological survey relating to ground water, by Oscar E. Meinzer, (Water supply paper 427.) Wash., D. C., Govt. print. off., 1917. 169p.

U. S. Geological survey. Index to the Hydrographic progress reports of the U. S. Geological survey, 1888–1903. by John C. Hoyt and B. D. Wood. (Water-supply paper 119.) Wash., D. C., Govt. print. off., 1905. 253p.

U. S. Geological survey. Preliminary index to river surveys made by G. S. and other agencies, by B. E. Jones and R. O. Helland. (Water supply paper 558.) Wash., D. C., Govt. print. off., 1926. 108p.

Wills

Fulton, Eleanore Jane and Barbara Kendig Mylin. Index to the will books and interstate records of Lancaster Co., Pa., 1729–1850. Lancaster, Pa., 1936. 136p.

Magruder, James M., comp. Index of Maryland colonial wills, 1634–1777. Annapolis, Md., The compiler. 3v.

Wisconsin — History

Wisconsin magazine of history. Madison, State historical soc. Index, v. 1–15, 1917–1931.

Wisconsin state historical society. Collections. Madison. Index, v. 1–20, 1854–1911.

Wisconsin state historical society. Proceedings. Index, no. 1–49, 1874–1901.

Wood

American wood preserver's association. Chicago. Proceedings. Index, v. 1–25, 1905–1929.

Wood preserving news. Chicago, Amer. wood preservers' assoc. Index, v. 1–8, 1923–1930.

World War

See **European War, 1914–1918.**

Zoology

Biological bulletin . . . including Zoological bulletin, *see* **Biology.**

Cushman laboratory for foraminiferal research. Contribution. Sharon, Mass. Index, v. 1–5, 6–10, 1925–1934.

Manual of conchology. Philadelphia. Index, v. 2–17, 1880–1897/98.

National institute of health. Historical catalogue, index catalogue of medical and veterinary zoology, by C. W. Stiles and Albert Hassall. (Bulletin 140, 142, 148, 150, 152, 155.) Wash., D. C., The institute, 1925.

U. S. Bureau of animal industry. Index-catalogue of medical and veterinary zoology . . . by Albert Hassall . . . and Maggie Potter. Wash., D.C., Govt. print. off., 1932. pt. 1; Also pts. 2, 3, 4, 5.

APPENDIX

Frequency Table;
The Use of Indexes in Reference Work

The Frequency Table has been compiled in order to indicate the approximate frequency with which the various indexes are used in reference work. Questionnaires were sent to a representative number of libraries including public, college and university, state, and teachers' training institutions. Returns were received from 23 different states.

We asked that the indexes be rated according to five separate categories (*see* Table, below), in order that the indexes could be more easily and accurately classified. No list of indexes was attached to the questionnaires, and according to the limitations of our work (see Preface, viii) no foreign publications were to be included. Altho there was some variance in type classification of titles, we have taken this fact into consideration in computing points and the results are as statistically accurate as possible.

Some factors must be considered in the interpretation of the Table, however, for instance the low rating of a few books which seemingly should be higher. There are several reasons for this, one of which is the strict interpretation of the word "index" which caused many reference librarians to omit quotation books, for example (*see* Preface, vii). Yet, on the other hand, some titles were listed which we did not include in our work. Another factor which made a difference in the rating of some titles was the departmentalization of large libraries, which made classification difficult. Then, too, some special subject indexes, such as those in children's literature, are not usually found in a general reference room.

In addition to the titles included in the Frequency Table, there were of course many others which received a smaller number of votes. 218 indexes were submitted in all, but since only 70 were requested we have only included that number in our final Table.

AN INDEX TO INDEXES

I. Special Indexes

	Points	Page
1. Granger—Index to poetry and recitations	713	56
2. Sears and Shaw—Essay and general literature index	529	23
3. Firkins—Index to short stories	510	65
4. Firkins—Index to plays	414	18
5. Sears and Crawford—Song index	325	66
6. Sutton—Speech index	280	68
7. Logasa and VerNooy—Index to one-act plays	260	18
8. Monro and Cook—Costume index	206	16
9. Bruncken—Subject index to poetry	193	56
10. Silk and Fanning—Index to dramatic readings	191	62
11. Ellis—General index to illustrations	189	56
12. Lovell and Hall—Index to handicrafts	161	30
13. Logasa—Biography in collections	134	8
A. L. A. Portrait index	134	57
14. Mallett—Index of artists	130	5
15. Hefling and Dyde—Index to contemporary biography	115	8
16. Bibliographic index	113	7
17. Stevenson—Home book of quotations	107	60
18. Price and Ticen—Index to vocations	99	73
19. Ireland and Ireland—Index to monologs and dialogs	93	45
20. Bartlett—Familiar quotations	88	58
21. Minneapolis public library—Index to folk dances	85	25
22. Ellis—Nature index	77	56
23. Hazeltine—Anniversaries and holidays	75	31
24. Sears—Standard catalog for public libraries	66	10
25. Lingenfelter—Vocations in fiction	64	72

II. Indexes to Sets of Books

1. Encyclopedia Britannica	311	21
2. Cambridge history of English literature	175	39
3. Encyclopedia of the social sciences	173	66
4. Dictionary of American biography	149	8
5. Hastings—Encyclopedia of religion and ethics	135	63
6. Mythology of all races	99	47
7. Cambridge history of American literature	88	39
8. Dictionary of American history	85	30
9. Catholic encyclopedia	83	13
10. Phelps—Debate index	73	17
11. National cyclopedia of American biography	70	8
12. Cambridge modern history	66	30
13. Frazer—The Golden bough	54	47
14. Dictionary of national biography	49	8
15. Moulton—Library of literary criticism	36	6

III. Periodical Indexes

1. Reader's guide	290	53
2. Book review digest	133	9
3. Industrial arts index	131	53
4. Education index	95	19
5. International index	91	53
6. Agricultural index	75	2
7. Public affairs information service	63	58
8. Magazine subject index	58	53
9. Art index	57	5
10. Poole's index	41	53

AN INDEX TO INDEXES

IV. Cumulative Indexes to Individual Periodicals

		Points	Page
1.	National geographic magazine	234	27
2.	New York times index	122	49
3.	Fortune (annual)	59	11
4.	Antiques	42	4
5.	American academy of political and social science—Annals	37	66
6.	Life (annual)	35	56
7.	Time (annual)	23	54
	American chemical society—Chemical abstracts	23	14
8.	American historical review	16	30
9.	Foreign affairs	15	33
	American journal of sociology	15	66
10.	St. Nicholas	9	15

V. Government Document Indexes

		Points	Page
1.	U. S. Dept. of agric.—Index to Farmers' bulletins	142	3
2.	U. S. Supt. of doc.—Monthly catalog of U. S. pub. documents	121	29
3.	U. S. Dept. of agric.—Index to publications	98	3
4.	U. S. Supt. of doc.—Price lists	86	29
5.	U. S. Supt. of doc.—Catalogue of the public documents	82	29
6.	U. S. Geological survey—Catalogue and index	41	28
7.	Congressional record (annual)	34	70
8.	U. S. Supt. of doc.—Checklist	31	29
9.	Poore—Descriptive catalogue	23	29
10.	U. S. Office of education—List of publications	22	20

AUTHOR-TITLE INDEX

	Page
A. L. A. Board on library service to children and young people. Sub-committee Subject index to children's plays	15
A. L. A. Booklist. *See* Booklist	
A. L. A. Index (and Supplement)	39
A. L. A. Portrait index	57
A. S. M. E. *See* American society of mechanical engineers	
A. S. T. M. standards and tentative standards	21
Abraham Lincoln association. Annual papers	39
Abridged Reader's guide to periodical literature	53
Abstracts of bacteriology, 1917–1925	6
Acacia (fraternity). Publications	25
Academy of natural sciences of Philadelphia. Index to the scientific contents of the Journal and Proceedings	63
Academy of science of St. Louis. Transactions	64
Accountants' index	1
Acoustical society of America. Journal	1
Actuarial society of America. Transactions	33
Addisonia	10
Aeronautical reader's guide	2
African repository	16
Agricultural index	2
Albertson, G. H. Geologic index (and Supplement)	27
Aldred, Thomas. Sequel stories	65
Allen, F. J. Guide to the study of occupations	72
Allibone, S. A. Great authors of all ages	58
Allibone, S. A. Poetical quotations from Chaucer to Tennyson	58
Allibone, S. A. Prose quotations from Socrates to Macaulay	58
Alphabetical index of occupations and industries	73
Alphabetical subject index and index encyclopedia of periodical articles on religion	63
Altsheler, Brent. Natural history index-guide	47
America's town meeting of the air. *See* Town meeting	
American academy of political and social science. Annals	66
American anthropological association. General index	4
American antiquarian society. Proceedings	4
American architect and the architectural review	5
American association of collegiate registrars. Journal	71
American association of instructors of the blind. Proceedings	9
American association of law libraries. Index to legal periodicals	37
American association of museums. Publications	46
American association of petroleum geologists. Publications	54
American association of teachers colleges. Yearbooks	71
American association of university professors. Bulletin	71
American bar association. Journal	37
American biography, a new cyclopedia	7
American book prices current	10
American bureau of geography. Bulletin	27
American Catholic historical society of Philadelphia. Records	13
American Catholic quarterly review	13
American ceramic society. Ceramic abstracts	13
American ceramic society. Transactions	13
American chemical journal. *See* American chemical society. Journal	
American chemical society. The chemical abstracts	14
American chemical society. Journal	14

AN INDEX TO INDEXES 79

American colonization society. Annual report............................ 16
American council of learned societies devoted to humanistic studies. Bulletin 31
American council on education. Studies................................. 19
American digest. Descriptive word index................................ 36
American digest tables of cases... 36
American economic association. Publications........................... 19
American federationist... 34
American fisheries society. Transactions............................... 24
American folk-lore society. Memoirs................................... 24
American foreign service journal....................................... 71
American foundrymen's association. Transactions....................... 25
American gas institute. Proceedings.................................... 54
American genealogical index.. 25
American geographical society of New York. Bulletin................... 27
American geographical society. Current geographical publications...... 55
American geologist... 28
American historical association. Annual report........................ 30
American historical association. Union list of collections in European history 30
American historical review... 30
American institute of accountants. Accountant's index (And Supplements).. 1
American institute of actuaries. The record........................... 33
American institute of architects. Proceedings......................... 5
American institute of chemical engineers. Transactions................ 14
American institute of electrical engineers. Transactions.............. 20
American institute of mining and metallurgical engineers.............. 44
American Jewish historical society. Publications...................... 34
American journal of anatomy.. 4
American journal of archaeology.. 4
American journal of education.. 19
American journal of hygiene.. 32
American journal of international law.................................. 33
American journal of mathematics.. 41
American journal of numismatics.. 49
American journal of nursing.. 49
American journal of orthopsychiatry.................................... 41
American journal of philology.. 35
American journal of physical anthropology.............................. 4
American journal of physiology... 56
American journal of psychology... 58
American journal of science.. 64
American journal of sociology.. 66
American journal of theology... 62
American labor legislation review...................................... 34
American law reports annotated. Complete word-index of annotations in
  American law reports... 36
American leather chemists association. Journal........................ 14
American library annual.. 6
American library directory... 67
American machinist... 40
American management association. The management index................ 11
American marine standards commission. American marine standard lists and
  indexes.. 48
American mathematical society. Bulletin............................... 41
American mathematical society. Transactions........................... 41
American medical association. Journal................................. 41
American microscopical society. Transactions.......................... 43
American mineralogist.. 44
American monthly microscopical journal................................. 43
American museum of natural history. Bulletin.......................... 47
American museum of natural history. Memoirs........................... 47

American nation series.. 30
American observer medical monthly.................................... 41
American oriental society. Journal.................................... 50
American pharmaceutical association. Proceedings..................... 55
American philatelist.. 55
American philosophical society. Proceedings.......................... 55
American philosophical society. Serial list of publications.............. 55
American philosophical society. Transactions.......................... 55
American political science review..................................... 57
American prefaces.. 39
American prison association. Proceedings of the annual congress........... 57
American railway bridge and building association. Proceedings........... 21
American railway master mechanics' association. Report of proceedings..... 69
American review of tuberculosis...................................... 41
American schools of oriental research. Bulletin....................... 50
American society for metals. Transactions............................ 44
American society for testing materials. Index to A.S.T.M. standards....... 21
American society for testing materials. Index to the literature on spectrochemical analysis.. 14
American society for testing materials. Proceedings..................... 21
American society of agronomy. Journal............................... 2
American society of civil engineers. Transactions...................... 15
American society of mechanical engineers. Transactions................ 41
American society of municipal engineers and International association of public works officials. Proceedings.. 46
American society of naval engineers. Journal......................... 48
American society of refrigerating engineers. Transactions.............. 62
American sociological society. Papers................................ 66
American statesmen series.. 8
American statistical association. Journal............................. 68
American surgical association. Transactions.......................... 41
American transit association. Summary index of Proceedings............ 69
American transit engineering association. Proceedings................. 70
American water works association. Proceedings....................... 73
American wood preservers' association. Proceedings................... 74
Americana. *See* Encyclopedia Americana
Americana annual.. 21
Ames, J. G. Comprehensive index to the publications of the U. S. government 28
Amos, Alice M. Where to find the new trade names.................... 69
Analytical bibliography of universal collected biography................. 8
Analytical index to the ballad-entries in the registers of the Company of stationers of London.. 6
Anatomical record... 4
Andover review.. 55
Anglican theological review... 62
Annals... 66
Annals of English literature.. 39
Annals of Iowa.. 33
Annals of mathematical statistics..................................... 68
Annals of mathematics... 41
Anniversaries and holidays... 31
Annotated bibliography of economic geology........................... 28
Annotated bibliography of mental tests and scales..................... 69
Annotated bibliography of 373 studies in agricultural education........... 2
Annotations of cases decided by the Supreme court of the U. S............ 35
Annual library index... 39
Annual literary index.. 39
(Annual) magazine subject index..................................... 53
Annual monitor... 25
Annual register... 30

AN INDEX TO INDEXES 81

Antiques.. 4
Appalachia.. 46
Appalachian coals, incorp. Proceedings...................... 44
Apperson, C. L. English proverbs and proverbial phrases..... 58
Archaeological papers....................................... 5
Architectural record.. 5
Archives of otology... 41
Army air corps information circulars........................ 44
Army and federal specifications............................. 43
Army regulations and changes................................ 44
Art index... 5
Artist's index to Stauffer's American engravings............ 5
Association of American geographers. Annals................. 27
Association of American medical colleges. Proceedings....... 41
Association of American physicians. Transactions............ 41
Association of life insurance council. Table and index of papers.. 33
Association of life insurance presidents. Proceedings....... 33
Association of official agricultural chemists. Journal...... 2
Astor library. Supplement to the Astor library catalogue.... 9
Astronomical society of the Pacific. Publications........... 5
Astronomy and astro-physics................................. 6
Astrophysical journal....................................... 6
Athenaeum subject index to periodicals...................... 53
Atlantic monthly.. 54
Auk, a quarterly journal of ornithology..................... 51
Author index to A Guide to material on crime and criminal justice... 16

B. A. E. news... 22
Bailey, L. H. Standard cyclopedia of horticulture........... 2
Bailey, Lois, comp. *See* Southwest review
Baker, B. M., comp. Dramatic bibliography................... 18
Baker, E. A. and James Packman. Guide to historical fiction. 24
Baker, E. A. and James Packman. Guide to the best fiction.. 23
Ballad books and ballad men................................. 6
Balzac, Honoré. *See* Gillette, F. B. Title index to the works.
Baring-Gould, Sabine. Lives of the saints................... 63
Bartlett, John. Familiar quotations......................... 58
Basic reference books....................................... 62
Becker, W. J. Metal projects index.......................... 30
Beautiful thoughts from French and Italian translations..... 60
Beautiful thoughts from German and Spanish authors.......... 60
Beautiful thoughts from Greek authors....................... 60
Beautiful thoughts from Latin authors....................... 60
Bell laboratories record.................................... 69
Bell system technical journal............................... 69
Belton, J. D. Literary manual of foreign phrases and classical quotations.... 58
Benham, W. G. Benham's book of quotations................... 58
Benham, W. G. Cassell's classified quotations from authors.. 59
Bennett, Wilma, comp. Occupations and vocational guidance... 72
Bent, S. A. Familiar short sayings of great men............. 59
Bernice Pauahi Bishop museum. Pacific entomological survey. Publications.. 22
Best books.. 10
Bibelot... 39
Bible... 62
Biblical world.. 62
Bibliographia genealogica Americana......................... 26
Bibliographic index... 7
Bibliographic review and index of papers.................... 73
Bibliographic review and index of underground water literature... 73
Bibliographical society of America. Index to the publications.... 7

Bibliographies and summaries in education............................ 19
Bibliography and index of geology exclusive of North America............ 28
Bibliography of aeronautics.. 2
Bibliography of American biography.................................... 8
Bibliography of American historical societies.......................... 30
Bibliography of costume... 16
Bibliography of librarianship... 38
Bibliography of library economy....................................... 38
Bibliography of mental tests and rating scales......................... 69
Bibliography of research studies in education......................... 20
Bibliography of speech education...................................... 68
Bibliotheca sacra... 62
Billboard stage... 69
Biographical index of American artists................................ 5
Biographical index of deceased British and Irish botanists............ 10
Biography by Americans.. 8
Biography in collections.. 8
Biological abstracts.. 8
Biological bulletin... 8
Biological society of Washington. Proceedings......................... 9
Bird-lore... 51
Black, A. D., comp. Index of the periodical dental literature......... 17
Black Hills engineer.. 21
Blom, Eric. A general index to modern musical literature.............. 47
Boggs, R. S. Index to Spanish folktales............................... 24
Bohn, H. G. Handbook of proverbs...................................... 59
Bohn, H. G. Polyglot of foreign proverbs.............................. 59
Bolton, H. J., comp. *See* Catholic historical review
Book-auction records.. 10
Book prices current... 10
Book review digest.. 9
Booklist.. 9
Books about jobs.. 73
Books index... 9
Boone, C. L. Guide and index to work and play books................... 30
Booth, M. J. Index to material on picture study....................... 56
Boston. Museum of fine arts. Bulletin................................. 46
Botanical abstracts... 11
Botanical gazette... 11
Botanical review.. 11
Boulger, G. S. *See* Britten, James, jt. comp.
Bowman, Border. Indexed digest of patent cases........................ 51
Boyce Thompson institute for plant research, inc. Contributions....... 11
Bradley, M. A. *See* U. S. Dept of agriculture. Index to publications, inc.
Brahm, W. T. Bibliography and index of publications of Western Reserve university.. 71
Brewer, D. J. World's best essays..................................... 23
Brewer, D. J. World's best orations................................... 50
Brewton, J. E. Index to children's poetry............................. 15
Bridger, Charles. Index to printed pedigrees.......................... 26
Britannica. *See* Encyclopedia Britannica
Britannica book of the year... 21
British museum. Subject index of the books relating to the European war... 23
British museum. Subject index of the modern works..................... 9
Britten, James and G. S. Boulger. Biographical index of deceased British and Irish botanists.. 10
Broom, Herbert. A selection of legal maxims........................... 37
Brown, S. J. M. International index of Catholic biographies........... 13
Browne, N. E., ed. *See* A. L. A. Portrait index
Browning, P. E. *See* Smithsonian institution. Index to the literature

AN INDEX TO INDEXES 83

Bruncken, Herbert. Subject index to poetry............................. 56
Bryan, W. J. and F. W. Halsey. World's famous orations................ 50
Bryologist... 11
Buros, O. K. *See* Educational, psychological and personality tests
Buros, O. K. *See* Mental measurements yearbook
Burr, Allston. Sir Walter Scott.. 39
Burton, Margaret and M. E. Vosburgh. Bibliography of librarianship...... 38
Business and trade directories... 18
Business directories... 17
Business education index... 12
Butler, N. M., ed. *See* Educational review

California. University. Publications in American archaeology........... 5
California. University. Bureau of public administration. Governmental research organization in the western states................................ 29
California law review.. 37
Cambridge history of American literature............................... 39
Cambridge history of English literature................................ 39
Cambridge modern history... 30
Canadian periodical index.. 12
Cannon, Clarence. Cannon's Precedents of the House of representatives of the U. S.. 51
Cannons, H. G. T. Bibliography of library economy...................... 38
Cannons, H. G. T. Classified guide to 1700 annuals, directories........ 17
Carey, A. E., P. R. Hanna and J. L. Meriam. Catalog, units of work..... 71
Carnegie endowment for international peace. *See* International conciliation
Carroll, H. C., comp. *See* U. S. Bureau of mines. Index of papers
Carroll, M. J. Key to League of nations documents...................... 37
Cassell's classified quotations.. 59
Casualty actuarial society. Proceedings................................ 33
Catalog of copyright entries... 16
Catalog, units of work... 71
Catalogue and index of contributions to North American geology......... 28
Catalogue and index of the publications of the Hayden, King, Powell and Wheeler surveys... 28
Catalogue of the public documents of Congress.......................... 29
Catholic encyclopedia.. 13
Catholic historical review... 13
Catholic library world... 38
Catholic periodical index.. 13
Catholic world... 13
Caudell, A. N. *See* Currie, Rolla, jt. auth.
Cavanaugh, E. S. *See* Special libraries, directory
Cement and engineering news.. 21
Central conference of American rabbis. Yearbook........................ 34
Central law journal.. 37
Century. *See* Forum and century.
Ceramic abstracts.. 13
Ceramic industry... 13
Ceramic literature... 13
Chambers, Sir Edmund. *See* White, Beatrice, comp. Index to the Elizabethan stage and William Shakespeare.
Champion, S. G. Racial proverbs.. 59
Chandler, F. R., ed. Indexes to the Bible.............................. 62
Channing, Edward. History of the United States......................... 30
Chapin, W. D. Index to original communications in the medical journals of the United States and Canada....................................... 41
Charities review... 65
Chase economic bulletin.. 19
Check list of biographical directories................................. 7

84 AN INDEX TO INDEXES

Checklist of U. S. public documents	29
Chemical abstracts	14
Chemical patents index	52
Chemical reviews	14
Chicago pathological association. Transactions	52
Child health bulletin	14
Children's poetry index	15
Children's short story index for special holidays	15
Children's song index	15
Chipman, G. E. *See* Jones, L. A., jt. auth.	
Christian examiner	62
Christy, Robert. Proverbs, maxims and phrases of all ages	59
Cincinnati society of natural history. Journal	47
Classical and foreign quotations	60
Classical journal	16
Classical philology	35
Classical weekly	16
Classics of American librarianship	39
Classified guide to 1700 annuals, directories, calendars and yearbooks	17
Classified index of materials	61
Cleveland engineering society. Journal	21
Clinical abstracts	42
Colcord, Mabel, comp. Index to the literature of American economic entomology	22
Cole, E. A. Check list of biographical directories	7
Cole, G. W., ed. Index to bibliographical papers published by the Bibliographical society	7
Collection of Chinese proverbs	60
Colonial society of Mass. Publications	40
Colophon	9
Colorado. University. University of Colorado studies	71
Columbia law review	37
Columbia University. Legislative drafting research fund. Index digest of state constitutions	35
Combined indices to the authors and titles of books and chapters in four collections of Buddhistic literature	63
Commerce clearing house. *See* Legal periodical digest	
Commissioner of education, Index to reports	20
Commonwealth review	50
Complete R. C. L. index	37
Complete word-index of annotations in American law reports	36
Comprehensive index. *See* U. S. Supt. of documents. Catalogue of the public documents	
Comprehensive index to the publications of the U. S. government	28
Comprehensive subject index to universal prose fiction	24
Comprehensive treatise on inorganic and theoretical chemistry	14
Compton's pictured encyclopedia	21
Compton's pictured encyclopedia *See also* War volume	
Concise poetical concordance	59
Condor	51
Congregational quarterly	63
Congressional committee hearings	70, 71
Congressional record	70
Consolidated index. *See* U. S. Supt. of documents. Index to the reports and documents	
Consolidated index to the Reported decisions of the I. C. C.	12
Conspectus incunabulorum	32
Constitution of the United States of America (annotated)	35
Constitutions of the states and United States	36
Consular reports	12

AN INDEX TO INDEXES 85

Contemporary American literature bibliographies and study outlines	40
Contemporary British literature bibliographies and study outlines	40
Cook, D. E. and E. C. Rahnek-Smith. Educational film catalog	46
Cook, E. T. and Alexander Wedderburn. General index to the works of John Ruskin	40
Cornell countryman	2
Cornell university. See Farm economics	
Corpus juris. Descriptive word-index	36
Corpus juris secundum	37
Costume index	16
Cotgreave, Alfred. Contents-subject index to general and periodical literature	53
Court-martial orders	48
Cowley, W. H. Personnel bibliographical index	54
Crane, E. J., comp. See American ceramic society. Transactions	13
Crane, W. R. Index of mining engineering literature	44
Crawford, Phyllis. See Sears, M. E., jt. ed.	
Crooks, Muriel. Essays on modern authors	6
Culver, Dorothy, comp. Author index to A Guide to material on crime and criminal justice	16
Cumulative book index	9
Cumulative index to a selected list of periodicals	53
Curiosities in proverbs	60
Current biography	8
Current geographical publications	55
Current legal thought	37
Current library literature	38
Currie, Rolla and A. N. Caudell. Index to circulars	22
Cushing, H. G. Children's song index	15
Cushman laboratory for foraminiferal research. Contributions	74
Cyclopedia of classified dates with exhaustive index	17
Dalbiac, Lilian. Dictionary of quotations (German)	59
Dalbiac, P. H. Dictionary of quotations (English)	59
Dalbiac, P. H. See Harbottle, T. B., jt. author	
Danvers historical society. Historical collections	40
Daughters of the American revolution. Lineage books	26
Daughters of the American revolution magazine. Subject index of lists of revolutionary soldiers	26
Davenport, D. H. and F. V. Scott. Index to business indices	11
Davenport academy of sciences. Proceedings	64
Day, E. P. Day's collacon	59
Dearmer, Percy. Subject index to hymns in the English hymnal	32
Debate index	17
Debate index supplement	17
Denison university. Scientific laboratories	64
Dental bibliography	17
Descriptive catalogue of government publications of U. S.	29
Descriptive-word index (Corpus juris)	36
Descriptive-word index to the 1st and 2d decennial digests	36
Dictionary of American biography	8
Dictionary of American history	30
Dictionary of applied chemistry	14
Dictionary of applied physics	56
Dictionary of best known quotations	59
Dictionary of biographical reference	8
Dictionary of contemporary quotations	61
Dictionary of foreign phrases and classical quotations	60
Dictionary of hymnology	32
Dictionary of Latin and Greek quotations	60

Dictionary of national biography	8
Dictionary of quotations (classical)	59
Dictionary of quotations (English)	59
Dictionary of quotations (French and Italian)	59
Dictionary of quotations (German)	59
Dictionary of quotations, Italian	59
Dictionary of quotations, Latin	59
Dictionary of similes	61
Dictionary of the Bible	63
Dictionary of thoughts	59
Digest of outstanding state legislation on agriculture	4
Dixson, Mrs. Z. A. Comprehensive subject index to universal prose fiction	24
Doctoral dissertations accepted by American universities	18
Documents relating to the colonial history of the state of New Jersey	48
Dodsley's annual register	30
Douglas, C. N. Forty thousand quotations	59
Dramatic bibliography	18
Dramatic index for 1909–date	18
Dramatist	18
Durfee, C. A. Concise poetical concordance	59
Durrie, D. S. Bibliographia genealogica Americana	26
Durrie, D. S. See Index to genealogies	
Dutchess co. historical society. Yearbook	48
Dyde, J. W. See Hefling, Helen, jt. auth.	
Early American periodical literature	53
Early Latin hymnaries	32
East, West, North and South in children's books	15
Eastman, M. H. Index to fairy tales	23
Ecclesiastical review	63
Eclectic magazine of foreign literature, science and art	54
Economic geology	28
Editorial research reports	54
Education	19
Education abstracts	19
Education index	19
Education, psychological and personality tests	69
Educational film catalog	46
Educational review	19
Edwards, Tryon. Dictionary of thoughts	59
Electric journal	20
Electric railway journal	70
Electrical world	20
Electrochemical society. Transactions	20
Elementary school journal. See Selected references in education	
Eliot, Charles W., ed. Harvard classics	40
Elisha Mitchell scientific society. Journal	64
Elizabethan stage and William Shakespeare	40
Ellis, J. C. General index to illustrations	56
Ellis, J. C. Nature index	56
Ellis, J. C. Travel through pictures	56
Ellis, Mary. Index to publications of N. Y. state natural history survey and N. Y. state museum	47
Employment service news	20
Encyclopedia Americana. See also Americana Annual	21
Encyclopedia Britannica. See also Britannica book of the year	21
Encyclopedia of religion and ethics	63
Encyclopedia of the social sciences	66
Engineering index	21
Engineering news-record	21

AN INDEX TO INDEXES

Engineering record	21
Engineer's society of Western Pennsylvania. Proceedings	22
English ballads and songs	6
English catalogue of books	9
English catalogue of books published 1801–1930	9
English proverbs and proverbial phrases	60
English proverbs and proverbial phrases, a historical dictionary	58
Essay and general literature index	23
Essays on modern authors	6
Essex antiquarian	26
Essex institute. Historical collections	40
Ethics	23
Events	54
Everett, L. D., jt. ed. *See* Bartlett, John. Familiar quotations	
Experiment station record	4
Factory mutual record	33
Facts on file	54
Familiar quotations	58
Familiar short sayings of great men	59
Famous sayings and their authors	60
Fanning, C. E. *See* Silk, A. K., jt. comp.	
Farm economics	2
Farmer's bulletins	3
Federal register	29
Federal reserve bulletin	11
Federal specifications	68
Felt, E. P., ed. *See* Colcord, Mabel, comp. Index to the literature of American economic entomology	
Field artillery journal	43
Film index	46
Finding list for United States patent, design, trade-mark, reissue, label, print, and plant patent numbers	52
Fire control notes	25
Firelands pioneer	50
Firkins, I. T. E. Index to plays (and Supplement)	18
Firkins, I. T. E. Index to short stories (and Supplements)	65
Flagg, C. A. Guide to Mass. local history	41
Fletcher, W. J., ed. *See* Poole's index to periodical literature (abridged)	
Florida historical society. The quarterly periodical	24
Fogle. F. R. *See* Patterson, F. A. An index to the Columbia edition of the works of John Milton	
Ford, James. ed. *See* Gries, J. M., jt. ed.	
Foreign affairs	33
Forest and stream	51
Forestry, current literature	25
Forestry quarterly. *See* Journal of forestry	
Fortune	11
Fortune, Vocational index to	73
Forty thousand quotations	59
Forum and century	54
Franklin institute. Journal	55
Frazer, J. G. Golden bough	47
French, Hebert, ed. Index of differential diagnosis	42
French review	25
Friends' historical society of Philadelphia. Bulletin	25
Frobisher, Martin, jr., comp. *See* American journal of hygiene	
Fulton, E. J. and B. K. Mylin. Index to the will books and interstate records	73
Gage, T. H. An artist's index to Stauffer's "American engravers"	5
Galloupe, F. E. Galloupe's general index to engineering periodicals	22

Genealogist's guide.. 26
General catalog of mariners' charts and books........................... 48
General index to illustrations... 56
General index to modern musical literature.............................. 47
General index to the published volumes of the diplomatic correspondence and foreign relations of the U. S..................................... 71
General orders.. 43, 44
General personal index of Journals of congress.......................... 70
Geographical review.. 27
Geographical society of Philadelphia. Bulletin........................... 27
Geologic index of the publications of the U. S. geological survey............ 27
Geological society of America. Bulletin................................. 28
Geophysical abstracts... 28
Geophysics... 28
Georgia historical quarterly... 28
Gilchrist, D. B., ed. Doctoral dissertations accepted..................... 18
Gillette, F. B. Title index to the works of Honoré de Balzac............... 40
Gilpatrick, E. M. Index of occupations................................ 72
Glazebrook, Sir Richard. Dictionary of applied physics................... 56
Golden bough... 47
Gomme, G. L. Index to archaeological papers.......................... 5
Goodtimes for all times... 51
Goulding, H. P., comp. *See* American book prices current
Goulding, P. S., comp. *See* American book prices current
Governmental research organization in the western states.................. 29
Granger, Edith. Index to poetry and recitations........................ 56
Granite monthly... 44
Gray, R. O. Index to 2500 books on industrial arts education............. 72
Great authors of all ages.. 58
Great debates in American history..................................... 17
Greathouse, C. H., comp. *See* U. S. Dept. of agriculture. Index to Farmer's bulletins
Green bag.. 37
Gries, J. M. and James Ford, ed. General index to the final reports of the President's conference on home building............................. 31
Griffin, A. P. A. Bibliography of American historical societies............. 30
Griffin, A. P. C. Index of articles upon American local history............. 30
Griffin, A. P. C. Index of the literature of American local history.......... 30
Grismer, R. L. A reference index to 12,000 Spanish-American authors...... 6
Grizzly bear.. 12
Guide and index to work and play books............................... 30
Guide to bibliographies of theses — United States and Canada............. 18
Guide to Catholic literature.. 13
Guide to historical fiction.. 24
Guide to magazine articles on industrial arts education................... 72
Guide to Mass. local history... 41
Guide to play selection.. 19
Guide to reference books (and Supplements)............................ 62
Guide to the best fiction... 23
Guide to the best historical novels.................................... 24
Guide to the study of occupations..................................... 72
Guides to business facts and figures................................... 12
Guthrie, A. L. *See* Saint Nicholas

Hall, R. M. *See* Lovell, E. C., jt. auth.
Handbook of proverbs.. 59
Hannigan, F. J. Standard index to short stories......................... 65
Harbottle, T. B. Dictionary of quotations (classical)..................... 59
Harbottle, T. B. and P. H. Dalbiac. Dictionary of quotations (French and Italian)... 59

AN INDEX TO INDEXES 89

Harbottle, T. B. and P. H. Dalbiac. Dictionary of quotations, Italian...... 59
Harbottle, T. B. Dictionary of quotations, Latin...................... 59
Harper's monthly magazine.. 54
Harper's weekly.. 54
Harris, Arthur, comp. *See* California. University. Bureau of public administration. Governmental research organization in the western states
Hartman, Dennis, ed. Income tax digest................................ 32
Hartman, Dennis, ed. Income tax index-digest.......................... 32
Hartman, Dennis, ed. Index of U. S. Board of tax appeals............... 32
Harvard annals... 6
Harvard business reports... 11
Harvard business review.. 11
Harvard classics... 40
Harvard graduates' magazine.. 71
Harvard law review... 37
Harvard theological review... 63
Harvard university. Harvard-Yenching institute. Combined indices....... 63
Harvard university. Harvard-Yenching institute. Index to thirty-three collections... 8
Harvard university. Library. Index of reference lists................. 7
Harvard university. Observatory. Bulletin............................. 6
Harvard university. Observatory. Harvard annals....................... 6
Harvey lectures.. 31
Harvey society. Harvey lectures...................................... 31
Hasid's index to periodicals and booklist............................ 34
Haskell, D. C., comp. *See* N. Y. Public library. Bulletin
Hassall, Albert. *See* National institute of health. Historical catalogue
Hassall, Albert. *See* U. S. Bureau of animal industry. Index-catalogue of medical and veterinary zoology
Hasse, A. R. Index of economic material in documents of the states....... 19
Hasse, A. R. Index to U. S. documents relating to foreign affairs.......... 33
Hastings, James. Dictionary of the Bible............................. 63
Hastings, James. Encyclopedia of religion and ethics.................. 63
Hawthorne, Nathaniel. *See* O'Connor, E. M. Analytical index to the works of
Hayden, H. L., comp. *See* Wood, James. Nuttall dictionary
Hayes, Rutherford B. *See* Ohio. Archaeological and historical society. Index and list of the pamphlets and periodicals
Hazeltine, A. I. Plays for children.................................. 15
Hazeltine, Mary. Anniversaries and holidays.......................... 31
Hazlitt, W. C. English proverbs and proverbial phrases............... 60
Heath, D. W. *See* American association of petroleum geologists. Publications
Hefling, Helen and J. W. Dyde. Index to contemporary biography and criticism... 8
Heidingsfield, M. S. *See* American statistical association. Journal
Helland, R. O. *See* U. S. Geological survey. Preliminary index to river surveys
Helps for club program makers.. 16
Henry, E. G. Helps for club program makers........................... 16
High points in the work of the high schools of N. Y. city............ 19
Highways.. 30
Hildreth, G. H. A bibliography of mental tests and rating scales..... 69
Hiler, Hilaire and Meyer Hiler. Bibliography of costume.............. 16
Hilton, Reginald, *see* Hutchesin, Sir Robert, jt. auth.
Hispania.. 67
Historical biographies... 8
Historical catalogue, index catalogue of medical and veterinary zoology..... 74
Historical fiction... 24
Historical society of Southern California. Publications.............. 12
History of nations... 31
History of the United States... 30
History reference bulletin... 31

History reference council. History reference bulletin...................... 31
Hockett, E. *See* American ceramic society. Transactions
Holmes, T. J. and G. W. Thayer. English ballads and songs............... 6
Home book of quotations.. 60
Home book of Shakespeare quotations.................................... 60
Homiletic review... 63
Hopkins, T. E. *See* Kinsev, V. E., jt. auth.
Horn book.. 15
Horne, C. F., ed. Source records of the Great War...................... 23
Hosea, H. R. *See* American statistical association. Journal
Housing index-digest... 31
Housing legal digest... 31
Hoyt, J. K. Hoyt's new encyclopedia of practical quotations............ 60
Hrdlicka, Ales. *See* American journal of physical anthropology
Hughes, E. H., ed. *See* Business education index
Hunt, M. G. *See* U. S. Dept. of agriculture. Index to Department bulletins
Hunt, M. G. *See* U. S. Dept. of agriculture. Index to Farmer's bulletins (no. 1–1500)
Hunter, W. L. and E. G. Livingston. Guide to magazine articles on industrial arts education and vocational industrial education..................... 72
Hustvedt, S. B. Ballad books and ballad men........................... 6
Hustvedt, S. B. Melodic index of Child's ballad tunes.................. 6
Hutchesin, Sir Robert and Reginald Hilton. Index of treatment.......... 42
Hyatt, A. L. Index to children's plays................................. 15
Hydrographic progress reports of the U. S. geological survey........... 73

Illinois law review.. 37
Illinois state academy of science. Transactions........................ 64
Illinois state federation of labor. Weekly news letter................. 34
Illinois state historical library. Collections......................... 32
Illinois state historical society. Journal............................. 32
Illustrative material for junior and senior high school literature..... 72
Income tax digest.. 32
Income tax index-digest of all court and treasury decisions............ 32
Index-abstract of surgical technique................................... 42
Index bibliographicus.. 38
Index-catalogue of medical and veterinary zoology...................... 74
Index digest of state constitutions.................................... 35
Index-digest of the Comptroller general of the U. S.................... 1
Index directory to special collections in North American libraries..... 67
Index librorum prohibitorum. Index of prohibited books................. 13
Index medicus.. 42
Index medicus ... War supplement....................................... 42
Index of ancestors and roll of members of the Society of colonial wars. 27
Index of articles upon American local history in historical collections. 30
Index of artists... 5
Index of celebrated cases, crimes...................................... 17
Index of data tabulated from the 1930 census of population............. 13
Index of differential diagnosis of main symptoms....................... 42
Index of economic material in documents of the states.................. 19
Index of legislation, 1890–1908.. 36
Index of literature from the publications of architectural societies... 5
Index of Maryland colonial wills....................................... 73
Index of mining engineering literature................................. 44
Index of periodical literature on testing.............................. 69
Index of prognosis and end-results of treatment........................ 42
Index of prohibited books.. 13
Index of reference lists and special bibliographies.................... 7
Index of symptomatology.. 43
Index of the literature of American local history..................... 30

AN INDEX TO INDEXES 91

Index of the periodical dental literature published in the English language... 17
Index of theses and dissertations prepared at Temple university............ 71
Index of treatment... 42
Index of twentieth century artists..................................... 5
Index psychoanalyticus.. 58
Index to all the publications of the Religious education assoc............... 63
Index to American Catholic pamphlets (and Supplements)................. 13
Index to American genealogies.. 26
Index to authoritative articles on every child rearing problem.............. 14
Index to bibliographical papers.. 7
Index to bibliographies and bibliographical contributions.................. 7
Index to business indices... 11
Index to children's plays... 15
Index to children's poetry.. 15
Index to collegiate business education.................................. 12
Index to contemporary biography and criticism.......................... 8
Index to dramatic readings... 62
Index to Early American periodical literature............................ 53
Index to fairy tales (and Supplement).................................. 23
Index to folk dances and singing games................................. 25
Index to genealogical materials in the Pennsylvania German............... 26
Index to genealogical periodicals...................................... 26
Index to handicrafts, modelmaking and workshop projects................. 30
Index to holiday plays for schools...................................... 15
Index to illustrations.. 56
Index to iron and steel patents.. 51
Index to kindergarten songs.. 15
Index to labor articles... 34
Index to Latin-American books....................................... 35
Index to legal periodicals, 1908–date................................... 37
Index to legal periodicals (Jones and Chipman).......................... 37
Index to library reports.. 39
Index to "Little classics" series.. 40
Index to material on picture study..................................... 56
Index to materials for study of Ohio history............................. 50
Index to monologs and dialogs.. 45
Index to names of persons and churches................................ 27
Index to occupations... 72
Index to occupations (Gilpatrick)...................................... 72
Index to one-act plays (and Supplement)............................... 18
Index to original communications in the medical journals................. 41
Index to parties... 51
Index to plays (and Supplement)...................................... 18
Index to poetry and recitations.. 56
Index to printed pedigrees.. 26
Index to printed Virginia genealogies................................... 27
Index to reference lists published by libraries........................... 7
Index to reference lists published in library bulletins..................... 7
Index to short stories (and Supplements)............................... 64
Index to short stories (Salisbury)...................................... 15
Index to some sources of current prices................................. 57
Index to South African periodicals..................................... 53
Index to Spanish folktales.. 24
Index to stories of hymns.. 32
Index to subject bibliographies in library bulletins....................... 7
Index to subject catalog of the technology dept.......................... 68
Index to the early printed books in the British museum................... 33
Index to the early printed books in the British museum (1501–1520 and Supplements)... 10
Index to the executive communications made to the House................ 70

Index to the federal statutes... 36
Index to the literature of gallium....................................... 45
Index to the literature of germanium.................................... 45
Index to the literature of indium.. 45
Index to the literature of the spectroscope.............................. 67
Index to the literature on spectrochemical analysis....................... 14
Index to the names of 30,000 immigrant German, Swiss, Dutch and French into Pennsylvania... 26
Index to the teaching of bookkeeping and accounting.................... 1
Index to the teaching of business law................................... 12
Index to the teaching of general business............................... 12
Index to 33 collections of Ch'ing dynasty biographies..................... 8
Index to 2500 books on industrial arts education........................ 72
Index to U. S. documents relating to foreign affairs...................... 33
Index to vocations... 73
Indexed digest of patent cases.. 51
Indiana academy of science. Proceedings............................... 64
Indiana magazine of history.. 33
Industrial arts index... 53
Insect life.. 22
Institute of radio engineers. Proceedings.............................. 61
Inter-American book exchange. Index to Latin-American books........... 35
International association of industrial accident boards. Proceedings...... 1
International association of public works officials. *See* American society of municipal engineers. Proceedings
International catalogue of scientific literature.......................... 64
International conciliation... 52
International critical tables... 64
International encyclopedia of prose and poetical quotations.............. 61
International index of Catholic biographies............................. 13
International index to periodicals....................................... 53
International journal of ethics... 23
International military digest... 43
Iowa engineer... 22
Iowa engineering society. Proceedings................................. 22
Iowa state agricultural society. Report................................. 2
Ireland, D. E. *See* Ireland, N. O., jt. auth.
Ireland, N. O. Historical biographies................................... 8
Ireland, N. O. and D. E. Ireland. Index to monologs and dialogs.......... 45
Irrigation age.. 2
Italica.. 34

Jacobsen, E. C., comp. *See* South Dakota historical collections
Jacobus, D. L. Index to genealogical periodicals........................ 26
Jelliffe, S. E. *See* Journal of nervous and mental diseases
Jewish education.. 34
Jewish frontier.. 34
Jewish quarterly review.. 34
Johns Hopkins university, Biological laboratory. Studies.................. 9
Johnsen, J. E. Debate index supplement................................ 17
Johnston, W. D. and I. G. Mudge. Special collections in libraries.......... 67
Jones, B. E. *See* U. S. Geological survey. Preliminary index to river surveys
Jones, H. P. Dictionary of foreign phrases.............................. 60
Jones, L. A. and G. E. Chipman. Index to legal periodicals............... 37
Josephson, B. E., comp. *See* Mississippi valley historical review
Journal. *See also* under names of Associations
Journal of accountancy.. 1
Journal of American folklore 24
Journal of American forestry. *See* Journal of forestry
Journal of American history... 31

AN INDEX TO INDEXES 93

Journal of American institute of architects. *See* Index of literature from the publications of architectural societies
Journal of American insurance.. 33
Journal of bacteriology.. 6
Journal of biological chemistry....................................... 14
Journal of criminal law and criminology............................... 16
Journal of experimental medicine..................................... 42
Journal of farm economics... 2
Journal of forestry... 25
Journal of geography.. 27
Journal of geology.. 28
Journal of industrial hygiene.. 32
Journal of infectious diseases....................................... 42
Journal of medical research... 42
Journal of mycology... 11
Journal of nervous and mental diseases............................... 42
Journal of nutrition.. 49
Journal of pharmacology and experimental therapeutics................. 55
Journal of prison discipline and philanthropy......................... 57
Journal of school geography... 27
Journal of social hygiene... 65
Journal of speculative philosophy.................................... 55
Journal of the American statistical association....................... 67
Journal of the western society of engineers.......................... 22
Journal of urology.. 42
Judson, K. B. Subject index to the history of the Pacific Northwest and of Alaska.. 49
Julian, John. Dictionary of hymnology................................ 32
Junior members round table of the A. L. A., comp. *See* Library literature, 1921–1932

Kansas government journal... 34
Kansas university quarterly... 71
Kaplan, Louis, ed. *See* Review index
Keeling, Wilbur. *See* American assoc. of collegiate registrars. Journal
Kentucky state historical society. Register.......................... 34
Kersley, R. H. *See* Broom, Herbert. A selection of legal maxims
Key to League of Nations documents.................................. 37
Kindergarten-primary magazine....................................... 19
King, W. F. H. Classical and foreign quotations..................... 60
Kinsev, V. E. and T. E. Hopkins. Index to iron and steel patents...... 51
Kipling index... 40
Kitchen, H. B. *See* Soil science
Klager, Karoline. *See* U. S. Bureau of labor statistics. Monthly labor review
Koger, M. V. Index to the names of 30,000 immigrant German, Swiss, Dutch and French into Pennsylvania....................................... 26

Laboratories data... 33
Lamkin, N. B. Goodtimes for all times............................... 51
Lancaster Co. Historical society. Historical papers.................. 52
Landscape architecture.. 35
Lane, W. C., ed. *See* A. L. A. Portrait index...................... 56
Language... 35
Larsen, Palmer, comp. *See* U. S. Bureau of mines. Index to geophysical abstracts
Last words, real and traditional.................................... 60
Latham, Edward. Famous sayings and their authors.................... 60
Law and labor... 34
Lawrence, Schuyler, comp. *See* Pennsylvania German. Index to genealogical materials

AN INDEX TO INDEXES

Lawson, Helen. *See* Journal of industrial hygiene
Lazare, Edward, ed. *See* American book prices current
League of nations. Index bibliographicus............................... 38
League of nations. Economic committee. Index to the reports 38
League of nations. Financial committee. Index 38
League of nations. International committee on intellectual coöperation. Index to the minutes.. 38
League of nations. Permanent mandate commission. General index to the records.. 38
League of nations. Treaty series. General indexes 38
Lean, V. S. Lean's collectanea... 60
Leftwich, R. W. An index of symptoms................................. 42
Legal periodical digest... 37
Lenrow, Elbert. Reader's guide to prose fiction......................... 24
Lewisiana index... 26
Library index... 32
Library journal... 38
Library literature (and Supplements).................................... 38
Library magazine.. 38
Library of literary criticism.. 6
Library quarterly... 39
Library work cumulated... 39
Life.. 55
Lincoln library of essential information................................ 21
Lineage books.. 26
Lingenfelter, M. R. Vocations in fiction............................... 72
List of American dissertations printed.................................. 18
List of doctors' and masters' theses in education........................ 71
List of series and sequels for juvenile readers........................... 65
"Literary characters drawn from life," Index and key to................. 40
Literary manual of foreign phrases and classical quotations.............. 58
(Littell's) Living age.. 54
Little, C. E. Cyclopedia of classified dates............................. 17
"Little classics" series.. 40
Lives of the saints.. 63
Living age.. 54
Living age. *See also* Eclectic magazine
Locating books for interlibrary loan.................................... 67
Logasa, Hannah. Biography in collections.............................. 8
Logasa, Hannah. Historical fiction..................................... 24
Logasa, Hannah and Winifred VerNooy. Index to one-act plays. (And supp.) 18
London library. Subject index... 10
London. Stationers' company. An analytical index to the ballad-entries..... 6
London Times. *See* Times, London
Lovell, E. C. and R. M. Hall. Index to handicrafts...................... 30
Loyola educational index.. 19
Lynch, Abigail, comp. Classified index of materials..................... 61

McAuslan, W. A. Mayflower index...................................... 26
McBride's magazine... 54
McCormick, Nellie. *See* National research council. Highway research board. Proceedings
McCown, W. V. *See* National research council. Highway research board. Proceedings
Macdonald, R. M. E. *See* U. S. Fisheries bureau. Analytical subject bibliography
McEldowney, M. L., comp. *See* The Library quarterly
McPherson, M. R. Children's poetry index............................. 15
Machinery's encyclopedia.. 40
Magazine and the drama.. 18

AN INDEX TO INDEXES

Magazine of American history.................................... 31
Magazine of history... 31
Magazine of history. Extra numbers.............................. 31
Magazine subject index.. 53
Magruder, J. M., comp. Index of Maryland colonial wills......... 73
Mailing list directory.. 17
Mallett, D. T. Index of artists (international-biographical)..... 5
Management index.. 11
Manley, M. C. Business directories.............................. 17
Manly, J. M. and Edith Rickert. Contemporary American literature bibliographies.. 40
Manly, J. M. and Edith Rickert. Contemporary British literature bibliographies.. 40
Manual for the genealogist...................................... 27
Manual of conchology.. 74
Manual of forensic quotations................................... 60
Marcus, Ruth. See American schools of oriental research. Bulletin
Marshall, G. W. The genealogist's guide......................... 26
Martin, E. W., comp. See Georgia historical quarterly
Marvin, D. E. Curiosities in proverbs 60
Marvin, F. R. The last words, real and traditional.............. 60
Mass. Agricultural experiment station. Index of bulletins....... 3
Mass. Historical society. Proceedings........................... 41
Mathematics teacher... 41
Matteson, D. M. See American historical review
Matteson, D. M. See American nation series
Mayflower index... 26
Mead, Levon and F. N. Gilbert. Manual of forensic quotations.... 60
Mearns, James. Early Latin hymnaries............................ 32
Medical annual, general index................................... 42
Meggers, W. F. See American society for testing materials. Index to the literature on spectrochemical analysis
Meinzer, O. E. See U. S. Geological survey. Bibliography and index
Mellor, J. W. Comprehensive treatise on inorganic and theoretical chemistry. 14
Melodic index of Child's ballad tunes............................ 6
Memorabilia mathematica.. 60
Mental measurements yearbook................................... 69
Mentor... 54
Merchants' magazine and commercial review...................... 11
Meroney, W. P. See American sociological society. Papers
Metal progress... 44
Metal projects index... 30
Metals and alloys.. 44
Methodist review... 63
Metropolitan life insurance co. Statistical bulletin............ 33
Metropolitan museum of art. See N. Y. Metropolitan museum of art
Michigan. Historical commission. Historical collections......... 43
Michigan law review... 37
Microscopical bulletin and science news......................... 43
Miller, M. M. Great debates in American history................. 17
Miller, O. K. The Latch Key of My bookhouse..................... 15
Millett, F. B. See Manly, J. M. and Edith Rickert. Contemporary American literature
Milton, John. See Patterson, F. A. Index to Columbia edition of the works
Milwaukee. Public museum. Yearbook.............................. 46
Mind your business.. 46
Mining and metallurgical society of America. Bulletin........... 45
Mining world index of current literature........................ 45
Minneapolis public library. An index to folk dances and singing games..... 25
Minnesota historical society. Collections....................... 45

Minor, K. P. *See* Southern historical society. Papers
Minto, John, ed. Reference books (and Supplement).................... 62
Mississippi river commission. Reports................................ 45
Mississippi valley historical review.................................. 45
Missouri historical review... 45
Modern eloquence.. 50
Modern language association of America. Publications................ 35
Modern language notes... 35
Modern music.. 47
Monist.. 55
Monro, Isabel and D. E. Cook. Costume index........................ 16
Monroe, W. S. and Louis Shores. Bibliographies and summaries in education 19
Monthly catalog of U. S. public documents............................ 29
Monthly checklist of state documents................................. 29
Monthly labor review.. 34
Monthly record of educational publications........................... 20
Moody, K. T. Index to library reports............................... 39
Moore, E. G., comp. *See* Channing, Edward. History of the United States
Morgan, V. E. Vocations in short stories............................ 72
Moritz, R. E. Memorabilia mathematica.............................. 60
Morley, Christopher, ed. *See* Bartlett, John. Familiar quotations
Morley, L. H. and A. C. Kight. Mailing list directory................ 17
Morsch, L. M., ed. *See* Library literature, 1921–1932
Motion picture review digest... 46
Mott and Hindman. *See* New York (state). Constitutional convention committee. Constitutions of the states and United States
Moulton, C. W. Library of literary criticism of English and American authors. 6
Mudge, I. G. Guide to reference books (and Supplements).............. 62
Mudge, I. G. *See* Johnson, W. D., jt. auth.
Municipal index... 46
Musical quarterly... 47
Munsell. *See* Index to American genealogies
Munsell's genealogical index... 26
My bookhouse... 15
Mycologia... 11
Mylin, B. K. *See* Fulton, E. J., jt. auth.
Mythology of all races.. 47

Nachtman, A. N. Index to subject bibliographies in library bulletins........ 7
Nation.. 54
National academy of sciences. Publications........................... 64
National association of cost accountants. Bulletin.................... 1
National association of insurance commissioners. Proceedings.......... 33
National collegiate athletic association. Proceedings................. 16
National conference of charities. Proceedings........................ 65
National conference of social work. Proceedings...................... 66
National cyclopedia of American biography............................ 8
National education association of U. S. Index by authors, titles and subjects to the publications 19
National electric light association. Proceedings..................... 20
National fire protection association. Publications................... 24
National foreign trade council. A topical index of addresses.......... 11
National geographic magazine.. 27
National geographic magazine, Skadsheim topical index................ 27
National health library. *See* Library index
National institute of health. Historical catalogue................... 74
National occupational conference. Occupational index................. 72
National research council. Bulletin.................................. 64
National research council. International critical tables............. 64
National research council. Highway research board. Proceedings........ 30

AN INDEX TO INDEXES

National retail dry goods association. Controller's congress. Index of convention reports.. 11
National shade tree conference. Proceedings............................. 25
National speech arts association. Proceedings............................ 67
Natural history index-guide... 47
Nature index... 56
Nature magazine.. 48
Nebraska ornithologists' union. Proceedings............................ 51
Nelson, C., ed. *See* Educational review
Nelson, M. F., comp. *See* National education association of U. S Index by authors, titles and subjects
New England historical and genealogical register....................... 26
New England museum of natural history................................. 48
New England quarterly... 48
New England water works association. Transactions and Journal...... 73
New Englander.. 54
New Jersey historical society. Documents relating to the colonial history.... 48
New Jersey historical society. Proceedings.............................. 48
New McClure's magazine.. 54
New York academy of medicine. Dental bibliography................... 17
New York academy of science. Transactions............................ 64
New York botanical gardens. Journal..................................... 11
New York daily tribune index.. 49
New York genealogical and biographical record......................... 26
New York herald tribune. Books index.................................... 9
New York libraries.. 39
New York. Metropolitan museum of art. Annual reports................ 46
New York. Metropolitan museum of art. Bulletin........................ 46
New York public library. Bulletin.. 39
New York review.. 54
New York (state). Constitutional convention committee. (Mott and Hindman) Constitutions of the states and United States........................ 36
New York state historical association. New York history............... 48
New York state historical association. Proceedings..................... 49
New York state library. Index of legislation............................. 36
New York state museum. Annual reports................................. 46
New York state Natural history survey. Publications................... 47
New York times index.. 49
Newark, N. J. Library. Subject index to about 500 societies............ 66
Nickles, J. M. *See* American mineralogist
Nickles, J. M. and R. D. Miller. Bibliography and index of geology........ 28
Nield, Jonathan. Guide to the best historical novels..................... 24
Niles' national register... 31
Nolan, E. J., ed. *See* Academy of natural sciences of Philadelphia. Index to scientific contents of the Journal and Proceedings
Noland, L. E., comp. *See* Wisconsin academy of sciences, arts and letters. Transactions
Norfolk journal and guide.. 49
North American review... 54
North Carolina booklet... 49
North central association quarterly....................................... 19
North Dakota University. Quarterly journal.............................. 71
Northup, C. S. Register of bibliographies................................. 7
Notices of judgment.. 24
Nuttall dictionary of quotations... 61

Occupational index.. 72
Occupations and vocational guidance..................................... 72
O'Connell, J. W. *See* U. S. Dept. of labor. Cumulative loose-leaf index to the Proceedings of the International association of industrial accident boards and commissions

O'Connor, E. M. Analytical index to the works of Nathaniel Hawthorne.... 40
Official gazette (U. S. Patent office).................................. 52
Ohio archaeological and historical quarterly.......................... 50
Ohio state archaeological and historical society. Index and list of the pamphlets and periodicals collected by Rutherford B. Hayes................. 67
Ohio state archaeological and historical society. Ohio archaeological and historical quarterly... 50
Ohr, Elizabeth, comp. Stories and poems for opening exercises............ 15
Oklahoma academy of science. Proceedings 64
Old-time New England.. 4
O'Neill, E. H. Biography by Americans................................. 8
Open court.. 55
Opera plots... 50
Opthalmic record.. 42
Optical society of America. Journal................................... 50
Ordway, Albert. General index of the Journals of congress............... 70
Ordway, Albert. General personal index of Journals of congress.......... 70
Oto-laryngology... 42
Outlook for the blind... 9
Overman, W. D. Index to materials for study of Ohio history............ 50
Oxford dictionary of English proverbs................................. 60
Oxford medicine... 42

P. M. L. A. *See* Modern language association of America. Publications
Pacific entomological survey.. 22
Pacific northwest quarterly... 49
Pageant of America.. 31
Pahasapa quarterly. *See* Black Hills engineer
Paine, C. S., ed. *See* Review index
Palfrey, T. A. and H. E. Coleman. Guide to bibliographies of theses...... 18
Palmer's index to the Times newspaper................................. 49
Pan American union. Bulletin.. 51
Pan-therapist... 42
Parents' magazine. Index to authoritative articles on every child rearing problem.. 14
Parker, W. E. Books about jobs.. 73
Partisan review... 54
Patent office society. Journal.. 51
Patents issued from U. S. patent office 51
Patents relating to electricity granted................................ 51
Patterson, F. A. An index to the Columbia edition of the works of John Milton 40
Paulmier, Hilah, comp. An index to holiday plays for schools............ 15
Peddie, R. A. Conspectus incunabulorum................................. 32
Peddie, R. A. Subject index of books published........................ 10
Pence, J. H. The magazine and the drama............................... 18
Pennsylvania German. Index to genealogical materials 26
Pennsylvania school journal... 19
Periodical articles on religion....................................... 63
Personnel bibliographical index....................................... 54
Phelps, E. M., ed. Debate index....................................... 17
Phi Delta Kappan.. 25
Philistine, a periodical of protest................................... 54
Phillips, L. B. Dictionary of biographical reference.................. 8
Phillips, M. S. *See* U. S. Office of education. Bulletins
Philosophical review.. 55
Philosophical society of Washington. Bulletin......................... 55
Physical review... 56
Physiological review.. 56
Phytopathology.. 11
Pilcher, E. H. *See* Methodist review

AN INDEX TO INDEXES 99

Pittsburgh. Carnegie library. Debate index.................................. 17
Pittsburgh. Carnegie library. Index to subject catalog.................... 68
Pittsburgh. Carnegie library. Technical book review index.............. 68
Plays for children, an annotated index.. 15
Poet lore... 56
Poetical quotations from Chaucer to Tennyson............................ 58
Political science quarterly... 57
Polyglot of foreign proverbs.. 59
Poole, Mary, ed. *See* Poole's index to periodical literature (abridged).
Poole, W. F. Alphabetical index to subjects treated in the reviews......... 53
Poole, W. F. Poole's index to periodical literature (and Supplements)..... 53
Poole's index to periodical literature (reprint)............................ 52
Poole's index to periodical literature, abridged (and Supplements)......... 53
Poore, B. P. A descriptive catalogue of government publications........... 29
Popular science monthly.. 64
Population index... 57
Portfolio.. 54
Portraits in books.. 57
Potter, Maggie. *See* U. S. Bureau of animal industry. Index-catalogue of medical and veterinary zoology
Preble, E. A., comp. *See* Nature magazine
Precedents of the House of representatives.................................. 51
Preliminary index to river surveys.. 73
President's conference on home building and ownership................... 31
Price, Willodeen and Z. E. Ticen. Index to vocations...................... 73
Price lists... 29
Price sources.. 57
Priced index, 1923-1932... 10
Princeton review.. 71
Printed salesmanship... 63
Proctor, Robert. Index to the early printed books.......................... 33
Proctor, Robert. Index to the early printed books, 1501-1520 (and Supplements)... 10
Professional memoirs... 22
Prose quotations from Socrates to Macaulay................................ 58
Proverb... 61
Proverbs, maxims and phrases of all ages.................................... 59
Providence. Public library. Index to reference lists....................... 7
Providence. Public library. Index to reference lists published........... 7
Providence. Public library. Quarterly index to reference lists........... 7
Psyche... 22
Psychoanalytic review... 58
Psychological abstracts... 58
Psychological index.. 58
Public affairs information service.. 58
Public affairs pamphlets.. 58
Public health nursing... 49
Publications in American archaeology and ethnology....................... 5
Pursglove, E. M. *See* U. S. Bureau of labor statistics. Monthly labor review

Quaker records.. 25
Quarterly cumulative index medicus... 42
Quarterly index to reference lists in other libraries...................... 7
Quarterly periodical.. 24
Quigley, M. C. Index to kindergarten songs................................. 15

Racial proverbs... 59
Radio annual... 61
Radio daily. The radio annual... 61
Rahnek-Smith, E. C. *See* Cook, D. E., jt. auth.

Rainey, Mrs. L. H., comp. *See* Daughters of the American revolution magazine. A subject index of lists of revolutionary soldiers
Ramage, C. T. Beautiful thoughts from French and Italian.............. 60
Ramage, C. T. Beautiful thoughts from German and Spanish authors...... 60
Ramage, C. T. Beautiful thoughts from Greek authors.................. 60
Ramage, C. T. Beautiful thoughts from Latin authors.................... 60
Rand school of social science. Index to labor articles..................... 34
Randall, Merle and E. B. Watson. Finding list for United States patent.... 52
Reader's guide to periodical literature................................. 53
Reader's guide to prose fiction.. 24
Records of the past.. 5
Reference books (and Supplement)..................................... 62
Reference books of 1935–1937 (Mudge)................................ 62
Reference books of 1938–1940 (Winchell).............................. 62
Reference index to 12,000 Spanish-American authors..................... 6
Register of bibliographies of the English language....................... 7
Religious education association. Index to all the publications............. 63
Research abstracts.. 29
Research projects... 29
Review index... 9
Review of reviews... 53
Reviews of modern physics... 56
Rhys, Ernest, ed. *See* Dictionary of best known quotations
Richardson, A. M. Index to stories of hymns........................... 32
Richardson, E. C. An alphabetical subject index and index encyclopedia of periodical articles on religion.. 63
Richardson, E. C. Index directory to special collections................. 67
Richardson, E. C. An alphabetical subject index........................ 63
Riches, P. M., comp. Analytical bibliography of universal collected biography 8
Rickert, Edith. *See* Manly, J. M., jt. auth.
Rickmann, John, comp. Index psychoanalyticus........................ 57
Ridings, Reta. *See* Wyoming. University. Publications
Rieck, Waldemar. Opera plots.. 50
Riker, Dorothy, comp. *See* Indiana magazine of history
Riley, H. T. Dictionary of Latin and Greek quotations.................. 60
Robbins, F. E., comp. *See* Classical philology
Roberts, Louise, ed. *See* Hoyt, J. K. Hoyt's new encyclopedia of practical quotations
Rochester historical society. Publication fund series...................... 49
Rockefeller institute for medical research. Studies....................... 42
Rollins, H. E., comp. *See* London. Stationers' company. An analytical index to the ballad-entries
Rose, D. E., comp. *See* Illinois state academy of science. Transactions
Rubber chemistry and technology...................................... 14
Rue, Eloise. Subject index to books for intermediate grades............... 61
Rue, Eloise. Subject index to readers.................................. 62
Ruling case law. Complete R. C. L. index............................. 37
Ruskin, John. *See* Cook, E. T. and Alexander Wedderburn. General index to the works

St. Louis. City art museum. Bulletin.................................. 47
Saint Nicholas.. 15
Salisbury, G. E. and M. E. Beckwith. Index to short stories.............. 15
Saxton, E. F. The Kipling index...................................... 40
Scarborough, William. Collection of Chinese proverbs................... 60
Schmeckebier, L. F. *See* U. S. Geological survey. Catalogue and index of the publications of the Hayden, King, Powell and Wheeler surveys
School arts magazine... 5
School review... 19
School review. *See also* Selected references in education

AN INDEX TO INDEXES

Science research associates. *See* Vocational guide
Scientific American supplement.. 64
Scott, F. V. *See* Davenport, D. H., jt. auth.
Scott, Sir Walter; an index.. 39
Scottish family history.. 27
Scribner, B. F. *See* American society for testing materials. Index to the literature on spectrochemical analysis
Scribner's magazine... 54
Scribner's monthly.. 54
Sears, M. E. and Marian Shaw. Essay and general literature index........ 23
Sears, M. E. and Phyllis Crawford. Song index.......................... 66
Sears, M. E. and others. Stadnard catalog for public libraries.......... 10
Selby, P. O., comp. Index to collegiate business education............. 12
Selby, P. O., comp. Index to the teaching of bookkeeping............... 1
Selby, P. O., comp. Index to the teaching of business law.............. 12
Selby, P. O., comp. Index to the teaching of general business.......... 12
Selected references in education...................................... 19
Selection of legal maxims... 37
Selective service law... 64
Sequel stories, English and American.................................. 65
Serial list of publications of American philosophical society.......... 55
Service and regulatory announcements.................................. 4
Sewage works journal.. 65
Shaw, Marian. *See* Sears, M. E., jt. auth.
Shearer, A. H. *See* American historical association. Union list of collections in European history
Shepard, F. J. Index to illustrations................................. 56
Shively, E. T. Index to some sources of current prices................ 57
Shores, Louis. Basic reference books.................................. 62
Shores, Louis. *See* Monroe, W. S., jt. auth.
Short, A. R., ed. An index of prognosis and end-results of treatment.... 42
Silk, A. K. and C. E. Fanning, comp. Index to dramatic readings........ 62
Silk, A. K. and C. E. Fanning. Index to parties....................... 51
Sims, Richard. A manual for the genealogist, topographer.............. 27
Skadsheim topical index to the National geographic magazine........... 27
Sloane, Victoria, comp. *See* American journal of orthopsychiatry
Smith, M. M. Guide to play selection.................................. 19
Smith, R. C. Biographical index of American artists................... 5
Smith, T. C. General index to the American statesman series........... 8
Smith, W. G. Oxford dictionary of English proverbs.................... 60
Smithsonian institution. Catalogue of publications.................... 65
Smithsonian institution. Index to the literature of gallium........... 45
Smithsonian institution. Index to the literature of germanium......... 45
Smithsonian institution. Index to the literature of indium............ 45
Social science abstracts.. 66
Social service review... 66
Society for the preservation of New England antiquities. Old-time New England.. 4
Society for the promotion of agricultural science. Proceedings......... 3
Society for the promotion of engineering education. Proceedings....... 22
Society of American foresters. Appalachian section. Proceedings....... 25
Society of colonial wars. Index of ancestors.......................... 27
Society of exploration geophysicists. Publications. *See* Geophysics
Society of medical history of Chicago. Bulletin....................... 43
Society of motion picture engineers. Journal.......................... 46
Society of naval architects and marine engineers. Transactions........ 48
Society of petroleum physicists. Publications......................... 28
Soil science.. 66
Solon, L. M. E. Ceramic literature.................................... 13
Song index (and Supplement)... 66

102 AN INDEX TO INDEXES

Sonnenschein, W. S. The best books	10
Source records of the Great War	23
South, E. B. An index to periodical literature on testing	69
South African library association. Index to South African periodicals	53
South Dakota historical collections	67
Southern historical society. Papers	66
Southern literary messenger	40
Southwest review	67
Speaker	68
Special collections in libraries in the U. S.	67
Special libraries	39
Special libraries association. Business and trade directories	18
Special libraries association. Guides to business facts and figures	12
Special libraries association. Special libraries	39
Special libraries association. Trade names index	69
Special libraries directory	67
Special library resources	67
Speech index	68
Spenser, Edmund. *See* Whitman, C. H. Subject index to the poems	
Standard catalog for public libraries	10
Standard cyclopedia of horticulture	2
Standard index to short stories	65
State law and index and digest	36
Statistical data compiled and published	3
Statistics on Canadian commodities	68
Statistics on commodities	68
Stevens indicator	22
Stevenson, B. E. Home book of quotations	60
Stevenson, B. E. Home book of Shakespeare quotations	60
Stewart, R. A. Index to printed Virginia genealogies	27
Stiles, C. W. *See* National institute of health. Historical catalogue	
Stokes' encyclopedia of familiar quotations	61
Stories and poems for opening exercises	15
Street railway journal	70
Stuart, Margaret. Scottish family history	27
Subject index of books published	10
Subject index of General orders of the War dept	44
Subject index of lists of revolutionary soldiers	26
Subject index of research bulletins	29
Subject index of the books relating to the European war	23
Subject index of the London library	10
Subject index of the modern works added to the library	9
Subject index to about 500 societies	66
Subject index to aeronautical periodical literature	2
Subject index to books for intermediate grades	61
Subject index to children's plays	15
Subject index to high school fiction	24
Subject index to hymns in the English hymnal	32
Subject index to poetry	56
Subject index to readers	62
Subject index to the economic and financial documents	38
Subject index to the history of the Pacific Northwest	49
Subject index to the periodicals in science and technology	64
Subject matter index of patents for inventions granted in France	52
Subject matter index of patents for inventions issued	52
Subscription books bulletin	10
Supplement to the Astor library catalogue	9
Surgery, gynecology and obstetrics	43
Sutton, R. B. Speech index	68
Swan, Helena. Dictionary of contemporary quotations	61

AN INDEX TO INDEXES

Swem, E. G. Virginia historical index.	72
Synoptical index of the reports of the statistician.	4
Tables of and annotated index to the Congressional series.	29
Tauber, M. F. Index of theses and dissertations prepared at Temple university library.	71
Taylor, Archer. The proverb.	61
Teachers college, Columbia university. Teachers college bulletin.	71
Technical book review index.	68
Technical book review index (Pittsburgh, Carnegie library).	68
Thompson, G. F. See U. S. Animal industry bureau. Index to literature	
Thompson, G. F. See U. S. Dept. of agriculture. Index to authors with titles of their publications	
Thompson, G. F. See U. S. Dept. of agriculture. Synoptical index of the Reports of the statistician	
Thonssen, E. F., comp. Bibliography of speech education.	68
Thorndike, A. H. Modern eloquence.	50
Thorpe, Sir Edward. Dictionary of applied chemistry.	14
Tibbott, G. L. See International association of industrial accident boards. Proceedings	
Tidy, H. L., ed. Index of symptomatology.	43
Time	54
Times, London. Palmer's index to the Times newspaper.	49
Times, London. Quarterly index. (Official index).	49
Times, London. The Times diary and index of the war.	23
Toglia, V. G., comp. See Italica	
Toner, J. M. M. D. Index to names of persons and churches.	27
Tonne, H. A. List of doctors' and masters' theses in education.	71
Topical index of addresses on foreign trade.	11
Topical index of population census reports.	13
Toronto library. See Canadian periodical index	
Torrey botanical club. Bulletin.	11
Town meeting; bulletin of America's town meeting of the air.	61
Towner, I. L., comp. Classics of American librarianship.	39
Trade-marks issued from the United States patent office.	68
Trade names index.	68
Trade prices current of American first editions.	10
Trail and timberline.	46
Transit journal.	70
Travel through pictures.	56
Treasury.	63
Treaty information.	70
Treffry, E. E. Stokes' encyclopedia of familiar quotations.	61
Troy, Zeliaette, comp. See Boyce Thompson institute for plant research, inc. Contributions	
Trust bulletin.	70
Trust companies.	70
Tuckerman, Alfred. Index to the literature of the spectroscope.	67
Ulrich, C. F., comp. See Young wings	
Uniform crime reports.	16
U. S. Animal industry bureau. Index to literature.	3
U. S. Board of tax appeals decisions.	32
U. S. Bureau of agricultural chemistry. Index of publications.	66
U. S. Bureau of agricultural economics. The B. A. E. news.	22
U. S. Bureau of agricultural economics. Indexes to state official sources of agricultural statistics.	3
U. S. Bureau of agricultural economics. Insect life.	22
U. S. Bureau of animal industry. Index-catalogue of medical and veterinary zoology.	74

AN INDEX TO INDEXES

U. S. Bureau of census. Alphabetical index of occupations............... 73
U. S. Bureau of census. Index of data tabulated......................... 13
U. S. Bureau of census. Topical index of population census.............. 13
U. S. Bureau of employment security. Employment service news........... 20
U. S. Bureau of ethnology. General index, annual reports................ 23
U. S. Bureau of ethnology. List of publications......................... 23
U. S. Bureau of foreign and domestic commerce. Index to the Consular reports 12
U. S. Bureau of foreign commerce. List of available publications issued..... 12
U. S. Bureau of labor statistics. Cumulative index to bulletins............. 34
U. S. Bureau of labor statistics. Monthly labor review.................. 34
U. S. Bureau of labor statistics. Subject index of the publications.......... 34
U. S. Bureau of mines. Index of papers................................. 45
U. S. Bureau of mines. Index of publications........................... 45
U. S. Bureau of mines. Index to geophysical abstracts................... 28
U. S. Bureau of mines. List of publications............................. 45
U. S. Bureau of public roads. Library. Highways....................... 30
U. S. Bureau of reclamation. Index to 1st–20th Annual reports............ 66
U. S. Bureau of standards. Alphabetical index.......................... 68
U. S. Bureau of standards. Publications................................ 68
U. S. Bureau of standards. Supplementary list.......................... 68
U. S. Congress. House. Congressional committee hearings................ 70
U. S. Congress. House. General personal index of Journals............... 70
U. S. Congress. House. Patents committee. Index of reports............. 52
U. S. Congress. House. Index to the executive communications........... 70
U. S. Congress. Senate. Congressional committee hearings................ 71
U. S. Copyright office. Catalog of copyright entries..................... 16
U. S. Crop estimates bureau. Statistical data............................ 3
U. S. Dept. of agriculture. Index to authors with titles of their publications. 3
U. S. Dept. of agriculture. Index to Bulletins........................... 22
U. S. Dept. of agriculture. Index to Department bulletins................ 3
U. S. Dept. of agriculture. Index to Farmers' bulletins.................. 3
U. S. Dept. of agriculture. Index to publications........................ 3
U. S. Dept. of agriculture. Index to Technical bulletins.................. 3
U. S. Dept. of agriculture. Index to the Annual reports.................. 3
U. S. Dept. of agriculture. Index to the Yearbooks...................... 3
U. S. Dept. of agriculture. List by titles of publications................. 3
U. S. Dept. of agriculture. List of publications......................... 4
U. S. Dept. of agriculture. Synoptical index of the Reports.............. 4
U. S. Dept. of commerce. American marine standards comm. American marine standard lists and indexes...................................... 48
U. S. Dept. of commerce. Price sources................................ 57
U. S. Dept. of labor. Cumulative loose-leaf index....................... 1
U. S. Dept. of labor. Index of all reports issued by bureaus............... 34
U. S. Dept. of state. General index to the published volumes of the diplomatic correspondence and foreign relations of the U. S........................ 71
U. S. Dept. of state. Treaty information............................... 70
U. S. Engineer dept. Index to the Reports of the chief.................. 22
U. S. Federal bureau of investigation. Uniform crime reports............ 16
U. S. Federal emergency relief admin. Subject index of research bulletins and monographs.. 29
U. S. Federal trade commission. Index-digest........................... 12
U. S. Federal works agency. Index of research projects.................. 29
U. S. Federal works agency. Central housing comm. Housing index-digest.. 31
U. S. Federal works agency. Central housing committee. Subcommittee on law and legislation. Housing legal digest.................................. 31
U. S. Fisheries bureau. Analytical subject bibliography of publications...... 24
U. S. Food and drug administration. Notices of judgment................ 24
U. S. Forest service. Fire control notes................................. 25
U. S. Forest service. Forestry current literature........................ 25

AN INDEX TO INDEXES 105

U. S. General accounting office. Index-digest of the Comptroller general of the United States.............	1
U. S. General accounting office. Index to the published decisions..........	1
U. S. General land office. Index to Circulars and publications............	35
U. S. General land office. Index to Circulars and regulations...since 1930...	35
U. S. Geographic board. Index to the fifth report......................	27
U. S. Geological survey. Bibliographic review and index of papers..........	73
U. S. Geological survey. Bibliographic review and index of underground water literature......................	73
U. S. Geological survey. Bibliography and index of publications...........	73
U. S. Geological survey. Catalogue and index of contributions............	28
U. S. Geological survey. Catalogue and index of the publications of the Hayden, King, Powell and Wheeler surveys..............................	28
U. S. Geological survey. Catalogue and index of the publications of the U. S. Geological survey..............	28
U. S. Geological survey. Index to the Hydrographic progress reports.......	73
U. S. Geological survey. Index to Water supply papers...................	28
U. S. Geological survey. Preliminary index to river surveys...............	73
U. S. Hydrographic office. General catalogue of mariners' charts..........	48
U. S. Interstate commerce commission. Reports.......................	12
U. S. Laws, Statutes. Index to the federal statutes......................	36
U. S. Library of congress. Catalog division. List of American dissertations..	18
U. S. Library of congress. Division of aeronautics. Subject index to aeronautical periodical literature and reports..................................	2
U. S. Library of congress. Division of documents. Monthly checklist of state documents...........	29
U. S. Library of congress. Legislative reference service. Digest of outstanding state legislation of agriculture.......................................	4
U. S. Library of congress. Legislative reference service. State law index and digest to the legislation of the states...................................	36
U. S. National archives. Federal register..............................	29
U. S. National museum. List of publications............................	47
U. S. National planning board, National resources board, National resources comm. Subject index of reports.......................................	47
U. S. Naval institute. Proceedings....................................	48
U. S. Naval medical bulletin...	43
U. S. Navy dept. Cumulative index to Court-martial orders..............	48
U. S. Office of education. An annotated bibliography.....................	2
U. S. Office of education. Bibliography of research studies................	20
U. S. Office of education. Bulletins...................................	20
U. S. Office of education. Index to reports of Commissioner..............	20
U. S. Office of education. List of publications...........................	20
U. S. Office of education. Monthly record of educational publications.......	20
U. S. Office of education. Public affairs pamphlets.......................	58
U. S. Office of experiment stations. Experiment station record............	4
U. S. Patent office. Annual report of the Commissioner..................	52
U. S. Patent office. Index of patents..................................	52
U. S. Patent office. Index of patents relating to electricity................	52
U. S. Patent office. Index of trade-marks issued........................	69
U. S. Patent office. Official gazette...................................	52
U. S. Patent office. Subject matter index of patents for inventions granted in France..........	52
U. S. Patent office. Subject matter index of patents for inventions issued by the U. S. patent office..	52
U. S. Plant industry bureau. Contents of and index to the Bulletins of the bureau	4
U. S. Plant quarantine bureau. Cumulative index to Service and regulatory announcements........	4
U. S. Public health service. Publications...............................	32
U. S. Railroad labor board. Decisions.................................	61

U. S. Selective service system. Index to selective service law.............. 64
U. S. Smithsonian institution. *See* Smithsonian institution
U. S. Supt. of documents. Catalogue of the public documents............. 29
U. S. Supt. of documents. Checklist of U. S. public documents............ 29
U. S. Supt. of documents. Index to the reports and documents........... 29
U. S. Supt. of documents. Monthly catalog of U. S. public documents...... 29
U. S. Supt. of documents. Price lists................................... 29
U. S. Supt. of documents. Tables of and annotated index to the Congressional series... 29
U. S. Surgeon-general's office. Index catalogue of the library............. 43
U. S. Tariff commission. Subject index of Tariff publications.............. 68
U. S. War dept. Index of U. S. army and federal specifications............ 43
U. S. War dept. Index to General orders 43
U. S. War dept. Adjutant general's office. Analytical index to General orders 43
U. S. War dept. Adjutant general's office. Index to Army regulations 44
U. S. War dept. Adjutant general's office. Subject index of general orders.. 44
U. S. War dept. Office of Judge advocate general. Consolidated index of published volumes of opinions 44
U. S. War dept. Office of the chief of air corps. Index to unrestricted U. S. army air corps information circulars................................... 44
U. S. War dept. Ordnance bureau. Index to Ordnance pamphlets.......... 44
U. S. War dept. Ordnance bureau. Index to reports of the chief........... 44
U. S. Works progress administration. Bibliography of aeronautics.......... 2
U. S. Works progress administration. Research abstracts.................. 29
United States Catalog... 10
United States Daily.. 49
United States Reference publications.................................... 29
Universalist quarterly and general review................................ 63
University review... 72

Van Nostrand, Jeanne. Subject index to high school fiction............... 24
Van Patten, Nathan. An index to bibliographies......................... 7
Ver Nooy, Winifred. *See* Logasa, Hannah, jt. auth. Index to one-act plays
Vertical file service catalog.. 51
Virginia historical index... 72
Vocational guide.. 73
Vocational index to Fortune.. 73
Vocations in fiction.. 72
Vocations in short stories.. 72
Vormelker, R. L., ed. *See* Special library resources

Walbridge, Earle. Index and key to "Literary characters drawn from life".. 40
Wale, William. What great men have said about great men 61
Wallace, Eugenia, comp. *See* American book prices current. A priced index
Wallace, L. E. *See* American book prices current. A priced index
Walsh, W. S. International encyclopedia of prose and poetical quotations... 61
Wang, C. K. A. An annotated bibliography of mental tests............... 69
War volume of Compton's pictured encyclopedia......................... 23
Warman, P. C. *See* U. S. geological survey. Catalog and index of the publications
Warner library... 40
Washburn, Edward, ed. *See* National research council. International critical Tables
Washington University. Studies.. 72
Washington historical quarterly. *See* Pacific northwest quarterly
Water supply papers... 28
Wead, K. H. List of series and sequels for juvenile readers................ 65
Wedderburn, Alexander. *See* Cook, E. T., jt. auth.
Weinberger, B. W., comp. *See* New York Academy of medicine. Dental bibliography.
Wells, G. H. The works of H. G. Wells................................ 40
Wells, H. G. *See* Wells, G. H. The works

AN INDEX TO INDEXES

Wendelin, E. C. Subject index to the economic and financial documents of the League of Nations 38
Western city... 46
Western Reserve university. *See* Brahm, W. T. Bibliography and index of publications of Western Reserve university
Western society of engineers. Journal................................. 22
Weston, B. E., comp. *See* American library directory
What great men have said about great men............................. 61
Wheatley, H. B. Portraits in books................................... 57
Wheeling, Katherine and J. A. Hilson. Illustrative material for junior and senior high school literature.. 72
Where to find the new trade names...................................... 69
White, Beatrice, comp. Index to The Elizabethan stage and William Shakespeare.. 40
White's conspectus. *See* National cyclopedia of American biography
Whitman, C. H. Subject index to the poems of Edmund Spenser.......... 56
Wilcox, J. K. United States reference publications.................... 29
Will books and interstate records of Lancaster co..................... 73
Willging, E. P. The index to American Catholic pamphlets (and Supplement) 13
Wilson, F. H. Bibliography of American biography..................... 8
Wilson library bulletin... 39
Wilstach, F. J. Dictionary of similes................................. 61
Winchell, C. M. Locating books for interlibrary loan.................. 67
Winchell, C. M. Reference books of 1938–40............................ 62
Wire, G. E. Index of celebrated cases, crimes........................ 17
Wisconsin academy of sciences, arts and letters. Transactions........ 31
Wisconsin magazine of history.. 74
Wisconsin state historical society. Collections...................... 74
Wisconsin state historical society. Proceedings...................... 74
Wood, James. Nuttall dictionary of quotations........................ 61
Wood preserving news... 74
Worcester art museum. Bulletin....................................... 47
Worden, E. C. Chemical patents index................................. 52
World peace foundation. World peace foundation pamphlets............. 52
World's best essays.. 23
World's best orations.. 50
World's famous orations.. 50
Wright, E. A. *See* U. S. Office of education. Bulletins
Writer's program of the W.P.A. *See* The Film index
Wurzburgh, D. A. Children's short story index........................ 15
Wurzburgh, D. A. East, North and South in children's books........... 15
Wyoming. University. Publications.................................... 72

Yale law journal... 37
Yale literary magazine... 40
Yale review.. 54
Young wings.. 15

Z
6293
I7
1972

OCT 22 1973